The
UltiMATE
Woman

By Bea Basansky

LONGWOOD COMMUNICATIONS

Published by:
Longwood Communications
397 Kingslake Drive
DeBary, FL 32713
904-774-1991

To order additional copies or to have Bea Basansky speak to
your group, write to:

Love and Grace Fellowship, Inc.
P. O. Box 7126
Ft. Myers, Fl 33911-7126
813–768–1300

First printing	1979	Second printing	1980
Third printing	1982	Fourth printing	1986
Fifth printing	1993		

Dedication

To my precious husband, Bill, who loves me as Christ loves the Church and who has helped to make my life exciting and fulfilled.

To my sons who have brought joy to my heart and many opportunities to test my "home face" smile!

To my mother who loved me through many aches and pains, and taught me how to be a feminine woman.

To my dear friend Ruth Baker who has spent endless hours teaching wives "how" to love their husbands and with her godly knowledge was an especially great influence in my life.

Contents

"It's Our Secret"

When you begin to use the principles in this book, you want them to become a part of the new you. Don't run to your husband and "let him in" on all you have learned. If you do, he will think it is an act that won't last more than a couple of days. You don't want to give the enemy any chances to divide you like that. Let the Lord help you become the "new" you, and if He has revealed things that need changing within you, begin praying. Ask the Holy Spirit to help you to become one with your husband in the spirit, soul and body, making you "The UltiMATE Woman" in his life.

Don't be discouraged if you feel the first few chapters are a little heavy. As we lay the groundwork, read prayerfully and then I promise, as you get into it, it lightens up.

I Love You,

The UltiMate Woman

PART ONE

Our Ministry in the Spirit

Chapter One

Why, Lord?

T herefore, a man shall leave his father and his mother and shall become united and cleave to his wife, and they shall become one flesh" (Gen. 2:24; Eph. 5:31).

When we enter into a love covenant (contract, agreement) with our mate, each of us loses the right to an independent life-style. We have CHOSEN to become joined to their life. We no longer consider only self when making decisions, entertaining ideas or displaying attitudes and emotions.

Someone has said, "Marriage is like a violin. After the beautiful music is over, the strings are still attached."

Many couples have some kind of storybook imagination of what they think marriage is, should be and will be as they walk down the road of life together. Quite frankly, it seems that very few have discovered, or been taught the fact and seen the evidence, that all good marriages *are* good marriages because the husband and the wife both WORKED at it. It is not a good marriage just because we think of each other as beautiful or handsome, using all the other adjectives that we could find to suit our mate, or think because we have so much in common it's bound to be good.

The fact is: *working to make a marriage successful today is a most difficult endeavor, since the devil is in an all-out war to destroy happy marriages and happy homes.* He especially zeros in on Christian marriages because he wants to discredit the Word of God and to break down God's kingdom on earth.

You may rest assured of this fact: I do not think that the woman is the only one at fault in the marriage that fails. However, I know this, that even if it is "ALL his fault," most of the time YOU can bring that marriage into the type of relationship it ought to be, if you are willing to be honest with yourself and with God.

There is a great deal of power in a Holy Spirit-filled woman—power to turn every situation around for good! Remember: IT *IS GOD'S WILL* for your marriage to work and that is *why* you can have that power.

After coming to know the Lord in a personal way and being filled with the Holy Spirit, and after fifteen years of an up-and-down marriage, I was beginning to get some light on this marriage covenant which I have with my husband. I could acknowledge that we had both come to know the Lord Jesus Christ. This fellowship with Him was allowing us to come together in spirit, and that spirit area seemed to be well on its way to being fulfilled.

"But why, Lord? Why? Why do I keep jeopardizing this relationship?" I kept calling out on my knees in prayer and with many tears.

The Bible says, **"Seek** (actually the Greek here says 'keep on seeking') **and you will find"** (Matt. 7:7). The trouble with some of us is that we refuse to seek because the search starts to crucify "self " and it hurts!

Oh, if I can only convince you through this writing that you will have the most wonderful reward waiting for you if you will just USE THE EQUIPMENT God has given you: in your *spirit, soul* and *body*, and then stick it out until they do their work! We have seen beautiful results in just a matter of weeks with some who have put to work these principles which we are going to consider here; and their marriages just get better and better!

But then I have seen a few who had to stick it out for almost a year before the husband could believe that his wife had really changed, or before he, through her faithful encouragement, had picked up the responsibilities in their marriage to the point where the rewards became evident.

All of a sudden I could see those areas in which I kept falling short. It was in the BODY AND SOUL realms.

Many Christians do not understand the triune person that we are (spirit, soul and body), and because of this, have a great deal of trouble rightly dividing the Word of God, properly renewing their minds according to that Word and truly pinpointing where their problem areas are in life.

Discovering myself as a triune person caused my life to be totally revolutionized. My eyes were opened and now I could begin to see how I could get the help I so desperately needed in the BODY AND SOUL realms of my life. I became aware that my spirit, yielded to the Holy Spirit, *had* to be in control.

Each one of us desires to be a beautiful, intelligent, successful and vibrant woman in the eyes of our husband, boyfriend or even brother or father. We can learn how to have all of these attributes, learn to minister to all the different types of men who are in our lives, and we can find out **what kinds of needs a man has** and how we can relate to those needs.

As concerned Christians, we can plainly see that we have problems in our churches and homes and these, of course, equate with national problems. I know that there would not be as much adultery, crime, juvenile delinquency and all those other sins to which man succumbs, if every woman and man would really *be* "Spirit-filled." These problems could turn into mere situations through which to walk. We would have a whole creation of people who would be satisfied, whose needs would be met and who wouldn't be out looking for those needs to be met elsewhere.

It was also brought to my attention that here, right in my own community (of all the places, where we think that people would be happy because we are in the "Bible Belt of America"), there is raging a problem that has reached epidemic proportions. In fact, I could not believe the statistics which my ears were hearing until I listened to the man on the radio repeat it for the second time.

"In this calendar year, in Tulsa County," he said, "there were more divorces than marriages!"

My mind reeled. To be certain, I thought, the situation is no better today. I recalled several couples with whom we had recently counseled: "Spirit-filled Christians," yet having such gross problems that when we talked to them our hearts were filled with pain.

Then, talking to the Lord, I said, "Where are we missing it, dear Jesus? Here we are, supposedly a Christian community! No wonder the world looks at us and says, 'Hypocrites!'"

Then another thing came to mind. I realized that under the pressures which we have in our own lives and marriages, mainly with our own families, we end up reacting in the same way as our mom and dad did. Under pressure situations, we end up doing and saying the same things that they did and said, even though we once said in our own minds, "I would never do that!" Nevertheless, in tight pressure-strained situations in our marriage and family affairs, we end up doing the same things. The old reactions that were instilled into us in our homes before marriage and/or reactions because of sins against each other in our marriage (even though we have forgiven and forgotten those sins) have not been dealt with. The Word says that the sins (and faults) of the fathers are passed on to the third and fourth generations (see Deut. 5:9).

Could it be that we have not been taught that we must set up a defense mechanism (reactions) which would be edifying to those around us?

For the past two generations, we have had women who were expected to take male responsibility. I think this trend arose most during World War II. We had "Rosie the Riveter" who went to the aircraft factory and was really plugging in the rivets, freeing our men for military service. Women took over the work forces of America, and, in consequence, became very dominant, strong and responsible people. This moved many a wife right out of her natural role as "helpmeet" for her husband. It also established the fact that a woman can do almost anything she puts her mind (will) to do (which is not all bad but sometimes is not expedient).

Where many failed was when Johnny came marching home. Instead of releasing the responsibility to her returning husband and going back to her natural responsibilities, especially in the area of the home, many of them held onto the reins. **Just because we have the intellect, education or talent to do something does not always mean that we are justified in doing it.**

Right before this transition in the woman's role, we had two generations of pioneer women who were also very strong-willed women, able to hold up under much stress and strain. Yet there was still an attitude of submission in many of them that had not really left the woman and her role. She was still able to recognize the influence and value of her function in the home, and kept looking up to her mate as the leader.

It seems that after World War II something did happen to the American Woman: perhaps we could call it a bad case of pride. Of course, there were the men who dropped into the background (some because of war-weariness), forcing the woman to run the home. In the absence of the father, many of the children had already begun to run wild. With women taking the lead and men drawing back from their responsibilities as husbands and fathers, the situation in many families worsened.

Divorce became a commonplace solution to problems in a nation of people who, in times past, had seldom sought such an avenue of escape from their marital problems.

Now, in our present world, our children have been crying out, "Everything is plastic. Nothing is real!" As adults, we have received the challenge to show them and teach them what *is* real.

Receiving what I have to say as a woman to you will depend on three different things. *First of all,* your attitude—being WILLING to admit that your attitude toward yourself and your husband (and others of both sexes) *may* be wrong. You may have to admit that your marriage is not what it should be and that some of it could be your fault. Again, I am not saying that husbands don't have faults, but let us women examine ourselves first.

As Jesus said,

"For just as you judge and criticize and condemn others (your mate) **you will be judged and criticized and condemned, and in accordance with the measure you deal out to others** (your mate) **it will be dealt out again to you (Matt. 7:2,** parentheses mine).

We can learn how to plant good seeds so that we can reap a good harvest: in other words, CHANGE many of our husband's faults through being willing to change ourselves.

The second factor in receiving what I have to say will depend upon your position in Christ Jesus. Without Christ in our lives, it is impossible to make a perfected change or have a proper understanding of ourselves.

Without Christ, we cannot be adaptable, we have no real wisdom, we cannot forgive others and we cannot forgive ourselves. We must KNOW His cleansing power and His Holy Spirit power in us.

This divine ability to forgive constitutes my third point, because forgiveness is the key to receiving from God and receiving from other people. We already know from the Lord's Prayer that God will forgive us *even as* we forgive others.

Unforgiveness can be found as the root to many problems in people's lives—unforgiveness of others or unforgiveness of self. Often it is a case of not understanding the forgiveness that God gives to us through Jesus Christ. Sometimes it seems like the things which we have gone through in our lives are so big or so bad that there is no way God could forgive us.

So it is important that we look into God's Word (which we shall do later in this book), and that we KNOW that when we ask the Lord to forgive us of our sins He has been faithful to remove all of that sin from us. No matter what it is, whether it is unfaithfulness, murder, gossip, adultery, lying, fornication or whatever it is, He promises to forgive. If your heart has truly repented to the Lord (you have confessed your sins), then *you are forgiven.*

The next step is forgive yourself. God says that those confessed and forsaken sins are in the depths of the sea NEVER TO BE REMEMBERED AGAIN. And that is an ASTONISHINGLY BEAUTIFUL TRUTH!

I attended church but was not sure that I was a born-again Christian. For 35 years I was taught that there was God the Father, who sent His Son, who gave His life for my sins, but I never understood the word "forgiveness" and did not KNOW salvation. Consequently, I lived in the guilt of my sins, unable to get closer to God. It just boiled down to the fact that I was being destroyed physically and spiritually for the lack of knowledge in the Word. Titus 2:3–5 says:

Bid the older women similarly to be reverent and devout in their deportment, as becomes those engaged in sacred service, not slanderers or slaves to drink. They are to give good counsel and be teachers of what is right and noble, so that they will wisely train the young women to be sane and sober-minded—temperate, disciplined—and to love [their] (*own) husbands and [their] children; to be self-controlled, chaste (*pure), homemakers, good-natured (kindhearted), adapting and subordinating themselves to their husbands, that the Word of God may not be exposed to reproach—blasphemed or discredited.

*RSV, Interlinear Greek/English New Testament (Zondervan).

Now, there is a lot to be digested in that scripture. Paul talks about the older women teaching the younger women, training them to love their husbands and their children. Did you really ever think that you would need to be *trained* to love your husband? My first reaction when I read this was, "Trained to love my husband? I *do* love my husband!" However, this was a purely sensual, fleshly, soulish love, subject to self. But REAL love, we find, has to come from our born-again spirit, by the Holy Spirit, transmitted to our mind (soul) and manifested through our body. This is the work which His presence within accomplishes.

It is natural, soulish love, in contrast to the God-kind of love. The soulish love says "Frankie shot her man because he done her wrong!" The God-kind of love says:

"Love endures long and is patient and kind; love never is envious nor boils over with jealousy; is not boastful or vainglorious, does not display itself haughtily.

"It is not conceited—arrogant and inflated with pride; it is not rude (unmannerly), and does not act unbecomingly. Love [God's love in us] does not insist

on its own rights or its own way, for it is not self-seeking; it is not touchy or fretful or resentful; it takes no account of the evil done to it—pays no attention to a suffered wrong.

"It does not rejoice at injustice and unrighteousness, but rejoices when right and truth prevail.

"Love bears up under anything and everything that comes, is ever ready to believe the best of every person, its hopes are fadeless under all circumstances and it endures everything [without weakening]" (1 Cor. 13:4–7, AMP).

We are told to be chaste (pure), domesticated (homemakers), kind and submissive. I will talk about those things later on, relating them to our soul realm.

Let us look at the very last of that scripture in Titus. It reads,

"that the word of God may not be exposed to reproach—blasphemed or discredited."

That means that we can cast doubt on the Word of God when we have anything less than a successful home which says, "Look, I am a Christian."

A properly ordered home will cause the outsider to say, "Yes, I can see what you have. You have love, joy, peace and everything is working in your home. What is your secret? I want it to work in mine."

There is one thing that will *never fail* in the home or anywhere else, and that is LOVE. In 1 Corinthians 13:8 the Word says:

"Love NEVER fails—NEVER fades out or becomes obsolete or comes to an end."

Chapter Two

The Ice Woman

The spirit of man (that factor in human personality which proceeds immediately from God) is the lamp of the Lord, searching in all his innermost parts" (Prov. 20:27).

Because of the influence that the world has had on us, we have become what I would call ICE—"I" for Independent, "C" for Capable and "E" for Efficient. We are so independent, so capable and so efficient that we can just do *everything*—"Let's do it MY way!" It all adds up to self-righteousness, doesn't it?

This ICE-woman is one of the enemies, one of the snares that I got caught in, because I *had* to (I thought) become this person. I *had* to become Independent, Capable and Efficient for fifteen years of marriage when we lived without Jesus Christ because my husband handed me the paycheck and I ran our house. I ran everything, and I became exactly this woman—self-righteous, but *ice*, just as cold as a cucumber.

How does this make our men feel? I'll tell you what

it does to them. It makes them feel less than a man. It makes them feel futile, ineffectual and humiliated. It causes them to stop fulfilling their role and their responsibilities as a man. So, any time you can really say that your husband is not bearing his responsibilities, then you had better start looking at yourself. You may have picked up a few of his duties and become very self-righteous in the process.

As women we are asked to be very versatile in our homes and in the world today. To be truly happy we must learn to function in this versatility and yet maintain our basic role of womanhood, God's plan for woman.

Because we are triune beings, the first step to real success is learning how to let our spirit have control over our soul and our body. Let's look at our chart.

Our spirit is sometimes called "the hidden man of the heart." This is what some may call our conscience, and this is where we have fellowship and relationship with God our Father and our Lord Jesus Christ. This is also where we receive revelation from God our Father— in the spirit. This is the supernatural realm of our triune being. In the spirit we operate for "good" only after we have established a right relationship with God. That, of course, is our *born-again* experience: inviting Jesus Christ to come into our life and letting Him, by our free will, take control.

When our spirit is born again and is in right standing with God, we become the righteousness of God.

"For our sake He made Christ [virtually] to be sin Who knew no sin, so that in and through Him we might become [endued with, viewed as in and examples of] the righteousness of God—what we ought to be, approved and acceptable and in right relationship with Him, by His goodness" (2 Cor. 5:21, AMP).

Because we now have a right standing with God, our spiritual relationship begins—we are justified and

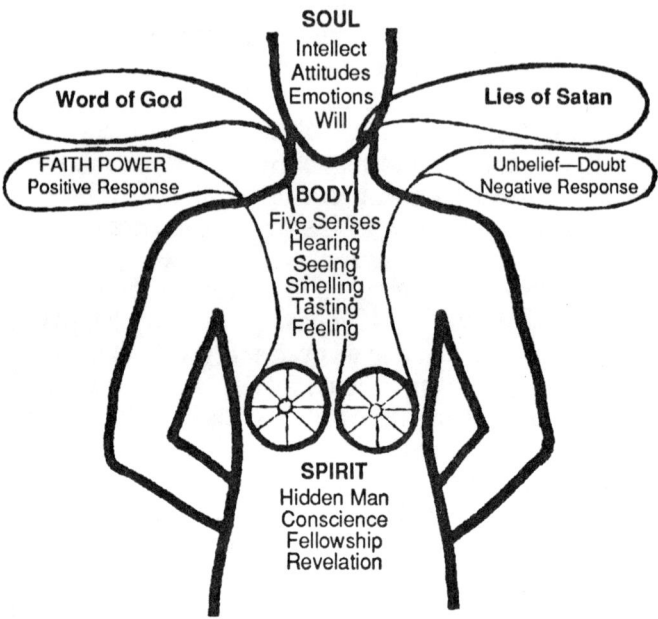

our spirit can now become stronger, bringing our soul and body into subjection and obedience to God's Word.

At this point it is imperative that a believer get into the Word of God, gaining a good knowledge of that Word. The Word is food for the spirit, and without it the spirit cannot become strong enough to reign over the soul and the body. In fact, we can literally be destroyed by the devil if we do not have a knowledge of the Word. Hosea 4:6 says,

"My people are destroyed for lack of knowledge."

If the church you are attending is a Bible-believing, Full Gospel church, then that should be your "church home." However, because God has set in the body of Christ ministry gifts, apostles, prophets, evangelists, pastors and teachers, it is good to seek them out. This will help to round out your spiritual education and also help to keep you from being caught up in the tradition and doctrines of men.

In all things which pertain to your life, whether it be spirit, soul or body, discern the spirit of the matter and check it out with the Word of God. If it is good it can stand the test. Two or more witnesses in the Word are always good safeguards which keep us from quoting Scripture out of context or from putting man's interpretation on it.

Of course, it is important to be *filled* with the Holy Spirit and to know the POWER (see Acts 1:8) of the Holy Spirit in our lives, with the evidence of speaking in tongues (see Acts 2:4). Some people have not yet come into the full manifestation of the infilling of the Holy Spirit, but I am sure that this is from the lack of understanding and teaching, because the Word says this gift is for everyone.

When we are filled with the Holy Spirit with the evidence of speaking in tongues, we come into a spiritual dimension—praying in the Spirit—in spirit and in truth just as we read in John 4:24. We WILL to pray in the Spirit (tongues) and to pray with our understanding (known language) according to 1 Corinthians 14:13–15.

After this, it is necessary to become sensitive to the guidance of the Holy Spirit. (In this regard, I recommend that you read my husband's book, *How to Know the Father's Voice*.) We need to develop in our spirit realm, becoming mature enough to know the difference between the Holy Spirit's guidance, our own mind and the voices of other spirits.

Once we are filled with the Holy Spirit, we can become spiritually aware of God's power, begin to recognize the power of demonic spirits and learn how to take authority over them. I know that this was true in my own life. It took the infilling of the Holy Spirit to show me the difference.

Please note now that many times I say "we need" certain things. I'm hoping when you see this *need* you will take the initiative to study God's Word to develop in these areas.

Faith in the spirit realm is needed also. We must have the God-kind of faith where we *know* that we *know* that ALL of our needs (spirit, soul and body) will be met in Christ Jesus (see Phil. 4:19). You ask, "Where do I get this faith?" Faith comes to us in our spirit realm first by hearing the Word of God, then it is transmitted to our soul and manifested in and through our body by word and deed:

1. In the spirit the seed is SOWN.
2. In the soul the seed is GROWN.
3. In the body the seed is SHOWN.

Next we must develop a willingness to be used in the gifts and ministries of the Lord. The Bible says to pray for the gift to prophesy (see 1 Cor. 14:1). Yet how many have prayed to prophesy? Many do not know that they are supposed to pray for the gifts, the nine gifts of the Holy Spirit, (see 1 Cor. 12:8–10).

All of the operations of these gifts come into our spirit by the Holy Spirit, working in accordance with the Word of God. Remember that all the gifts are for edification, exhortation and comfort.

The last thing in the spirit realm to which I shall refer is intercession in the Spirit for our families. That is one of the most important activities in which we need to operate as women. It is indeed one of our priorities. Intercession for our husband and for our children in the needs for their lives is a God-given responsibility to a wife and mother.

The next area of concern, then, is the soul realm. The soul is that part of us which comprises the intellect, the attitude, the emotions and the will. This constitutes the natural man, but the natural man can be influenced by the spiritual. Let us keep this in mind throughout our studies together. In the realm of the soul, a person with a renewed mind, the mind of Christ, will have the wisdom of God. They will have adaptability. They will be givers of love and transmitters of all the fruit of the Spirit which is found in Galatians 5:22–23.

This fruit is: love, joy, peace, patience, kindness, goodness, faithfulness, gentleness and self-control. If the fruit of the Spirit is to be genuine in your life, then it must be generated by the Holy Spirit through your spirit-man into your soul, and then be operating out of you through your body. It is not going to be the real thing, it is not going to be something that is really going to minister love, unless it is coming from your spirit-man, your reborn spirit which is in communion with God.

The fruit of the Spirit is *grown*—not acquired. You don't just all of a sudden have love, joy, peace, patience and so forth. You grow such fruit, allowing it to emerge from your spirit by the Holy Spirit into your soul realm and be manifested through your mouth, through your body.

A person with an unrenewed mind, then, would be that person with bad attitudes and bad emotions such as bitterness (which is self-pity gone wild), rebellion, resentment, unforgiveness. These are all products of the unrenewed mind. If you find yourself moving in any area of this nature even a little bit, you need to seek the Lord's help to remove these kinds of emotions and attitudes. Self-pity is one of the most tormenting spirits. It tormented me for years and years—self-pity and self-righteousness, they sort of go hand in hand—comrades, so to speak.

Immorality, selfishness, strife and idolatry—these are some of what the Bible calls the works (or deeds) of the flesh in Galatians 5:19–21. These come from the lusts of the flesh and from the world. Our soul can be fed, then, through our body, through the world, through the devil, or by our spirit (the Holy Spirit and the Word). We can have a renewed mind or an unrenewed mind as we choose. It is by the exercise of our will to wash our mind with the Word of God that we gain this renewed mind in Christ. It is going to take some work, but we are going to grow this fruit, because the Lord is going to show us how.

In Romans 12:1–2, Paul says,

"I appeal to you therefore, brethren, by the mercies of God, to present your bodies as a living sacrifice, holy and acceptable to God, which is your spiritual worship. Do not be conformed to this world, but be transformed by the renewal of your mind... "(RSV).

The last area with which we must deal then is the body. That is this vessel of flesh, bone and blood in which we live. We have the five physical senses in this body. We hear, we see, we smell, we taste, and we feel; and we also have our outward physical being, or personal appearance.

In the realm of the body and soul we are asked to perform as wives, lovers, mothers, cooks, chauffeurs, bookkeepers, secretaries, nurses, seamstresses, gardeners and so forth. You may be called to a career or to a ministry, or perhaps you have all these tasks as well as a ministry. That's being pretty versatile! Actually, just being a mother is quite a versatile calling in itself: asking her to perform in at least half of these occupations.

The world says, "You've come a long way, baby!" We see it expressed constantly in our magazines and newspapers, on television and everywhere we look—the epitome of the glamorous, competent and confident woman. We are tempted to think, "If I don't look just like that, then wow, I've missed it!" Of course, I think that most magazine models are beautiful, but in many I can see the world. Beneath the surface I detect the true woman that is concealed beneath the glamorous exterior.

We can be beautiful, and in fact, we are beautiful *and* glamorous when we allow our beauty to come out of our regenerated spirit, by the Holy Spirit. Through our regenerated spirit, we shall even know how to dress correctly as we will discuss in a later chapter.

Chapter Three

Satan's Fib

The women's liberation movement has had a loud voice in these last few years. A voice that cries that we are the same as men in many ways and should, therefore, have equal rights. There is a unisex spirit that is running rampant across America with homosexuality and lesbianism on the upsurge, influences which are causing men and women to fall into deep error.

"Adam's rib, Satan's fib made Women's Lib!"

The Women's Lib attitude has caused us to lose our men and has even gotten most of us to the place where we think the age of chivalry is really dead. I discovered that I had gotten to the place that I was feeling that way myself. When I first met my husband, chivalry was one of the first things that made me think he was one of the neatest guys on two feet: because he was opening doors and doing all of the polite things that a girl likes a guy to do for her. The things that make her feel protected and feminine. He was a real gentleman.

As the years went by, and I became that independent, capable and efficient woman, I was opening my own doors. I worked *myself* right out of that place where he could treat me gently.

Women's Lib has also put a few words in for good old Paul, and made us believe that he was a woman-hater. This is an insult to our intelligence as Spirit-filled, Bible-reading women. To prove it, I would like to show you a few scriptures where Paul honors women and the husband-wife relationship.

In Romans 16:1–2 he honored Phoebe as a deaconess of the church and commended her to the brethren to assist her in any business she had need of them because, he said, she had given aid to many and to Paul himself. In the same chapter, verses 3 and 4, he mentions Priscilla and Aquilla, wife and husband, who were his helpers to the point of risking their lives for him. In the sixth verse, he greeted Mary who, he said, had worked hard for them. In the twelfth verse there are Tryphena and Tryphosa. They were saluted by Paul for their labor in the Lord and were involved in a vital supportive ministry to him.

Now we can turn to Philippians 4:2–3 where he says,

"I entreat and advise Euodia and I entreat and advise Syntyche to agree and to work in harmony in the Lord. And I exhort you too, [my] genuine yokefellow, help these [two women, to keep on co-operating], for they have toiled along with me in [the spreading of] the good news (the Gospel), as have Clement and the rest of my fellow workers whose names are in the Book of Life."

In Ephesians 5:25, Paul exhorts the husbands to love their own wives as Christ loved the church. Here Paul is honoring the husband-wife relationship on a deep level. You know that Christ died for us, and Paul is exhorting the husbands to love and honor their wives as Christ loved the church. There is not a woman alive who does not want her husband to love her so much that he would lay down his life for her. That is inside every wife. We have that need inside us. It has to be fulfilled in order for us to really feel like our needs are met.

After reading these scriptures (and I know there are many more like them in the Bible), I can hardly conclude that Paul either enslaved or degraded any woman. They were working side by side with Paul.

Now, let us look at Jesus: how He talked about women. In the scriptures we find that He honored women. He showed gentleness, mercy and concern. We notice as Jesus traveled there were women with Him. First of all, we have Mary and Martha. They were the sisters of Lazarus. Jesus loved Mary and Martha and showed concern for them. That is clear from John, the eleventh and twelfth chapters.

In Mark 14:3–9, Mary's ministry to Jesus was so special that in verse nine He says,

"And surely, I tell you, wherever the good news (the Gospel) is proclaimed in the entire world, what she has done will be told for a memorial of her."

Because of her great love for Jesus, and because she moved by the prompting of her spirit, there was Jesus saying that wherever the Gospel would be preached, even two thousand years later, *Mary* would be honored because of the ministry she had done to Jesus.

We read in Luke 8:1–3 that Mary Magdalene, Joanna and Susanna traveled with Jesus and ministered to His needs out of their means. In John 19:26, Jesus was making sure that His mother, Mary, was taken care of. There are some who quote the scripture where the people came to Jesus and said, "Your mother wants to see you," to which He replied,

"My mother and my brothers are those who listen to the Word of God and do it! "(Luke 8:21).

The critics try to prove that Jesus was belittling His mother. That is not so. He was merely making the point that *at times* the service of God is more important than human relationships.

In John 4:7–42, we can read about the woman at Samaria. Jesus showed gentleness, mercy and concern for this woman who was full of sin. And through her testimony, many Samaritans came to know Jesus as Savior. The Bible doesn't say she became an apostle, prophet, evangelist, teacher and so forth. She just went back as the woman of Samaria and won her family and friends to the Lord, inspired by the love that He had shown to her.

If then, we have established that women *are* honored in the Bible, let us ask, "Why are women demanding equal rights?"

I believe that it is because we have abnormal situations such as broken homes, where a woman has *had* to take the responsibilities of a man. There are so many homes where men, for a number of reasons, will not accept responsibility. There are also situations where the wife has usurped the authority of the husband and is not allowing her husband to take the domestic headship.

I looked up the word "usurp" in the dictionary, and it says "to seize the rights or powers of another, without right or legal authority, take possession by force." Well, this is just what we find that many women have done today. I was guilty of it myself, which is why I know about it.

Now these are only some of the abnormal situations which abound. They are not all of them, I know, but this is the kind of society and culture that we are living in today—a culture of broken homes and lopsided roles of men and women.

I should say here that I *do* believe in equal rights for women in the labor market. A woman doing the same job as a man should receive the same pay and the same recognition for equal work. This is only logical, isn't it? But this is the one valid thing that Women's Liberation uses to bring in all the other issues that pervert the role of woman.

Women's Lib starts out presumably on the right

foot, you see, because there are some women who do have the sole responsibility of providing for a family or themselves. Why should they not make the same money for the same work? The injustice, however, has been played out of proportion. So if, and I say *if*, we want a good relationship with our men, we must go back to some of the very, very basic principles that are outlined in the Word of God.

We know that it takes the wisdom and knowledge which comes from God in dealing with man's spirit, soul and body. When our body and soul (that is, both the husband's and wife's) have been brought under subjection to the Word of God there is less ministry needed in the body-soul realm to our mate. Also, even as a mother, for example, we may have a lot of ministering in the body-soul realm to do to a son who has had his male ego (self-confidence) destroyed.

It would be great if all of us lived a spirit-controlled (by the Holy Spirit) life, but I don't see that happening in too many people's lives. A lot of us have come a long way, but most are not there yet. I wish that I could say, "I've arrived!" But I can say that I'm pressing toward the mark...and I am happy to say with Paul (Gal. 2:20),

"I have been crucified with Christ—[in Him] I have shared His crucifixion; it is no longer I who live, but Christ, the Messiah, lives in me; and the life I now live in the body I live by faith—by adherence to and reliance on and [complete] trust—in the Son of God, Who loved me and gave Himself up for me."

As we live this life in the body by and through FAITH in Him, we must *deal* with body-soul needs. As long as we are in the world, we will have to contend with the brainwashing that comes through the television, newspapers, magazines and so forth. A friend of mine called my attention to a scene she saw on television, showing a little girl walking across the floor in a room. She was, said the commentator, handicapped because she was a female!

You can imagine what kind of fear and confusion this manner of talk injects into our culture, into the young women of our country.

Of course, we know that wherever there is fear and confusion, this is the work of the devil. There are also things going on in the religious field, such as the extreme teachings on submission, that are bringing women into fear and confusion. Be alert! No matter what teaching you come across, if it brings fear and confusion, you had better start testing the spirits. The Holy Spirit does not minister fear and confusion.

Chapter Four

Are Women Equal with Men?

L et's examine, now, the question which is inherent in Women's Lib: Are women equal with men?

In the spirit realm I would say Yes! In the body and soul realms, I would say No! In the body realm there is a difference in our body structure, our physical strength, our mannerisms, the way we walk, the way we even throw our hands or our heads. Our entire role is different. It is femininity versus masculinity in the body realm.

In the soul realm, we see that women need love. They have a need for much verbal confirmation of their husband's love. They need more attention—attention-type of love, feeling cherished and protected. The woman takes the submissive role and the man takes the aggressive role by the God-given nature established from the beginning in the soul realm. In baseball terms, she becomes the "catcher" in relation to the man, who becomes the pitcher. He needs love too, but he needs it in these ways: through encouragement, admiration and through acceptance on our part. He has different needs because he has different responsibilities. He must have the place of honor in the body-soul realm.

The woman's role in the Old Testament appears to have been subservient, with honor basically obtained through childbearing. However, I think that has been overplayed in the light of women like Sarah, who stood with Abraham in strength and faith even when Abraham was wrong and God sided with Sarah because she was right; Queen Esther who saved her people, the whole nation of Israel, because of her wisdom from the Lord and her obedience; and Deborah, the prophetess who led and judged Israel. I would dare say that these last two, Esther and Deborah, were not subservient as they stood in their leadership roles.

Let us examine the first chart on domestic divine order. This is basically for order in the home.

First we have the Father, the eternal Godhead; then Christ Jesus the Head of the husband (or the wife, whichever is left in authority in the home). The husband, in the domestic divine order of the home, is the head of his *own* wife and children (see Eph. 5:23). I emphasize *own* because of some false teaching where some have said that *all* women should submit to *all* men (we shall discuss that later too).

A wife has authority over the children and is to be submissive to her husband (see Eph. 5:22). The children are to be submissive and obedient to their parents (see Eph. 6:1–3). This is DOMESTIC DIVINE ORDER. This is how we submit in the *body and soul realms* in a domestic situation.

Now, let's look at the second chart, SPIRITUAL DIVINE ORDER. *ALL* of us must go through Jesus to get to the Father. The children go up through Jesus to the Father. The wife (or woman) goes up through Jesus to the Father. The husband (or the man) goes up through Jesus to get to the Father. We *all* have our own

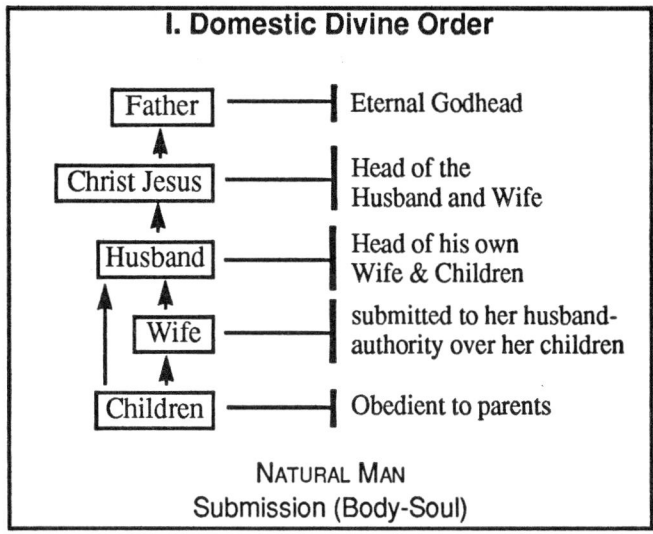

I. Domestic Divine Order

Father ——| Eternal Godhead

Christ Jesus —— Head of the Husband and Wife

Husband —— Head of his own Wife & Children

Wife —— submitted to her husband-authority over her children

Children ——| Obedient to parents

NATURAL MAN
Submission (Body-Soul)

individual EQUAL relationship—the *spiritual relationship* with God our Father through Jesus Christ. I think the reason there has been some false teaching in this area is because they have not rightly divided the Word (see 2 Tim. 2:15) into that which pertains to the domestic body and soul realms and that which pertains

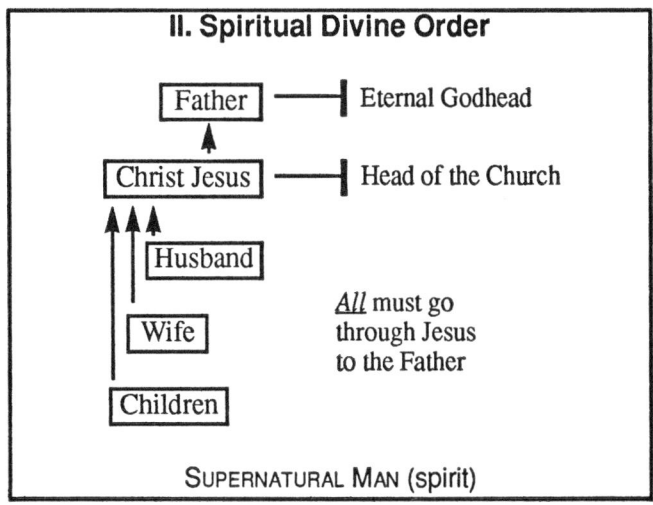

II. Spiritual Divine Order

Father ——| Eternal Godhead

Christ Jesus ——| Head of the Church

Husband

Wife   *All* must go
                     through Jesus
Children   to the Father

SUPERNATURAL MAN (spirit)

to the spirit realm. Some have said that a wife must go through her husband's domestic headship to get to Jesus and the Father. This is not the case. If it were, then a wife may be expected to go through an unbelieving husband who has no relationship with God. The woman or wife (born-again) has direct access to God at all times, as does the born-again husband or child.

Let us now turn to Genesis and take a look at Adam and Eve. I really got excited when I read Genesis and discovered how God looked down with compassion and saw that Adam had a need. He had a need for a helper. On the merit of that need, God made woman for man. He then ordained marriage and the home. In the Amplified, Genesis 2:18, He said,

"It is not good (sufficient, satisfactory) that the man should be alone; I will make him a help meet (suitable, adapted, completing) for him."

Another scripture that comes to mind is 1 Corinthians 11:7–9,

"For a man ought not to wear anything on his head [in church] for he is the image and [reflected] glory of God, [that is, his function of government reflects the majesty of the divine Rule]; but woman is [the expression of] man's glory [majesty, pre-eminence]. For man was not [created] from woman, but woman from man; neither was man created on account of or for the benefit of woman, but woman on account of and for the benefit of man."

That just really confirms what Genesis 2:18 says, doesn't it? God made woman for man. He made Eve for Adam.

We can see in Genesis 2:23 that Adam was simply delighted and said,

"This [creature] is now (implying AT LAST) bone of my bones and flesh of my flesh. She shall be called Woman, because she was taken out of man." (parentheses mine).

Adam really needed someone to be with him:

someone who could feel what he felt, smell what he smelled, touch what he touched, taste what he tasted, and love as he loved.

As I looked at that, I thought: here was Adam walking around in the Garden of Eden, with apparently every spirit, soul and body need met. He had a beautiful fellowship with God the Father. He talked with God. He had no barriers to break down, no sin, a beautiful garden to live in with all his material needs met and peace in his soul.

In spite of all that, God looked down and He said, "Man, you need a woman!"

God made woman and gave her to man as a "gift," knowing he had a body-soul need and this would complete him. When He gave her to Adam, as wife, it was like putting frosting on a cake; she became the "glory" of her man.

As we look at this body-soul relationship in a marriage, we see that a wife, from the beginning, was given a role under the authority of her husband, as a helpmeet. He was to lead and she was to support that leadership. Therefore we have to say in the marriage relationship (body-soul realm) she is unequal to her husband in domestic authority.

It seems the Sadducees were having difficulty separating body-soul functions from spirit when they came to Jesus with the hypothetical question, if a woman became the wife (and subsequent widow) of seven brothers in succession then whose wife of the seven brothers would she be in the resurrection? They were confused because they were trying to make a body application in the spirit realm. We find the answer to their problem in Mark 12:24–25 where Jesus said:

"Is not this where you wander out of the way and go wrong, because you know neither the Scriptures nor the power of God? For when they arise from among the dead, [men] do not marry nor are [women] given in marriage, but are like the angels in heaven."

He didn't say we would be angels, but would be like the angels in heaven. We are spiritual beings. So, Jesus was saying that in the spirit we are the same. There is not going to be any marriage in heaven, therefore, there is not going to be any husband-wife authority. There is not going to be any wifely submission—there's not going to be any need for it because that is domestic order for here on earth.

When Jesus came, He made the perfect and everlasting blood atonement for us, which enabled us to be born again. We were reborn in our spirit. Our spirit found eternal life with God (now we know that all spirits are eternal, but not all spirits have eternal life with God). You have to be born again so that your spirit can return to its original sinless form. That personal experience of the new birth is what makes a man and woman equal, but equal in the spirit, not in the body and soul. It is the new birth that makes us equal in the spirit and takes us out of the body-soul realm into the realm of the spirit. In Galatians 3:27–29 it says,

"For as many [of you] as were baptized into Christ—into a spiritual union and communion with Christ, the Anointed One, the Messiah—have put on (clothed yourselves with) Christ. There is [now no distinction], neither Jew nor Greek, there is neither slave nor free, there is not male and female; for you are all one in Christ Jesus. And if you belong to Christ (are in Him, who is Abraham's Seed), then you are Abraham's offspring and (spiritual) heirs according to promise."

Each one of us is an heir—not just the man, not just the woman. Each person who is born again in the spirit becomes that very person who is one with Christ, and heir according to the promise that was made to Abraham.

That did away with all the genealogies—the family trees—which all the people in the Old Testament had to maintain in order to establish that they were indeed

God's people. We know what we have and that we are God's people because of Jesus Christ, because through Him we have come together in the spirit realm, becoming the same, becoming one. First Corinthians 6:17 says,

"But the person who is united to the Lord becomes one spirit with Him."

So it is only in the spirit realm that we truly become equal with the male. This is true liberation. We are truly LIBERATED in Christ. The *body-soul relationship* requires subjection either to physical-natural laws or domestic order.

Chapter Five

Whose Head Is Who?

There are three scriptures I would like to share with you which witness that we are all the same—that we are all "sons." Now, sometimes that is hard for a woman to take! It's difficult for her to think that she is male, or a son, or should be called a son. Yet this is what we are in the spirit realm.

First, in Galatians 4:4 –7:

"But when the time had fully come, God sent forth his Son, born of woman, born under the law, to redeem those who were under the law, so that we might receive adoption as sons. And because you are sons, God has sent the Spirit of His Son into our hearts, crying 'Abba! Father!' So through God, you are no longer a slave, but a son, and if a son, then an heir" (RSV).

In Romans 8:14 –17 we read:

"For all who are led by the Spirit of God are sons of God. For you did not receive the spirit of slavery to fall back into fear, but you have received the spirit

of sonship. When we cry 'Abba, Father!' it is the Spirit Himself, bearing witness with our spirit that we are children of God, and if Children, then heirs, heirs of God and fellow heirs with Christ, provided we suffer with Him in order that we may also be glorified with Him (RSV)."

Again in 1 John 3:2 we read:

"Beloved, we are [even here and] now God's children, it is not yet disclosed (made clear) what we shall be [hereafter], but we know that when He comes and is manifested we shall [as God's children] resemble and be like Him; for we shall see Him just as He [really] is."

As long as we are in the body, we are male or female. But our spirits have equal authority and access to the spiritual things of God, and are classified neither male nor female.

How does this affect the question of submission and headship? In Genesis 2:18, we established that a woman was designed to be a helper for man. In Genesis 2:21–22, it says that woman was taken out of man's side (in order to walk alongside of him in the Christian manner). She was not taken out of his foot, to be trodden under and enslaved in the way of the heathen. God was saying in an allegorical way, "I am taking you, woman, out of Adam's side, and you are going to walk alongside him. He is not going to enslave you or use you for a doormat, wiping his feet on you, but you are going to be a help meet for the man." In Mark 10:6–9 we read,

"But from the beginning of creation, God made them male and female. For this reason a man shall leave his mother and father and be joined to his wife, and the two shall become one. So they are no longer two, but one. What therefore God has joined together let not man put asunder" (RSV).

This is the same scripture that is found in Genesis 2:24. It speaks of us coming together as one. It says that we become one flesh. We leave our original family and we become one flesh with our husband.

Not only do we come together in the body, which is the flesh, but we must come together in the soul and the spirit. We become one in each of those three realms. No two people could have a STRONGER AGREEMENT than when they agree as husband and wife. That is supreme POWER on earth when you come into one spirit with your husband. You can move MOUNTAINS!

Genesis 3:16 says,

"...Yet your desire and craving shall be for your husband, and he shall rule over you."

The dictionary definition of *rule* says, "to have influence (over); guide." This is God's Divine Order in the home. The husband is to rule over his wife. He is to be the head, and so this puts the wife in a submissive (not suppressed) role. The commandment fell upon Eve as a wife, not as a woman. Remember, you chose to join into this love covenant with your husband so you must abide by God's guidelines for that covenant. A woman is not subordinate, but a wife is. If you are in a home, a domestic situation with a husband, he is to rule over you. You are to be submissive and that puts you in a subordinate position.

But if you are a woman without a husband, you are not in a subordinate position. This means that *every man* DOES NOT rule over *every woman*. Certain "submission" teachings in the body of Christ have failed to see this fact and brought confusion and heartache into many lives. Just remember that it is a husband-wife proposition, and you won't get confused.

Wives must recognize their husband's domestic headship. We are to be submissive to him in the body and soul realms, and, if he is a believer, he should take over the spiritual leadership of the home.

There is a definite need for the mature women in the body of Christ to begin to teach our young women and daughters that when they make the decision to marry, they are saying to that man, "I am willing to submit myself to you according to the Word of God."

Submissiveness is not meant to be a cop-out for you. This is another place where some women have thought, "This is just super. If my man is supposed to take the spiritual leadership, then I'm not going to teach Sunday school anymore. I'm going to stop having devotions with my children. I'm going to stop teaching them spiritual things at home. I'm just going to let my husband do it all!"

They not only copped out in that area, but they said, "He can have the rest of the responsibilities too. I'll just sit here and be sweet and submissive."

That doesn't work either. That's a cop-out and cop-outs don't work. We *do* have responsibilities even though it is his place to take the leadership role. Some wives must accept more responsibilities than others depending on the husband's maturity and occupation. However, the *attitude* must remain submissive.

Now, if you are in a situation where your husband is an unbeliever, then he cannot possibly take the spiritual leadership role. It is up to you, for the sake of yourself and your children, to take this leadership. But if he is still in your household, this has to be done with care. You have to be very careful of the male ego, and do not intimidate him in his male leadership role. If he is not a believer, you can take the spiritual leadership, but you have to guard the body-soul relationship and his leadership there. It is through your ministry in the body and soul realms that the Lord can bring this man into salvation, since his spirit is still not alive to God.

"In like manner you married women, be submissive to your own husbands—subordinate yourselves as being secondary to and dependent on them, and adapt yourselves to them. So that even if any do not obey the Word [of God], they may be won over not by discussion but by the [godly] lives of their wives."

"When they observe the pure and modest way in which you conduct yourselves, together with your

reverence [for your husband. That is, you are to feel for him all that reverence includes]—to respect, defer to, revere him; [revere means] to honor, esteem (appreciate, prize), and [in the human sense] adore him; [and adore means] to admire, praise, be devoted to, deeply love and enjoy [your husband]" (1 Pet. 3:1–2).

We have heard much about women having to have a *covering*. A man's doctrine brought many women into bondage saying she must have a male spiritual head in authority over her. There is a difference between the spiritual Headship of Christ and the spiritual leadership of a husband, an elder or a pastor. We need to understand this difference.

"But I want you to know and realize that Christ is the head of every man, the head of a woman (wife) is her husband, and the Head of Christ is God" (1 Cor. 11:3, parentheses mine).

First of all, this means that Christ is our spiritual Head. He is the Head of a man and He is the Head of a woman. He is the *spiritual* Head. He is our covering because it is with His blood that He covered us, justified us and sanctified us.

In 1 Corinthians 7:13–14 we can see where either a man or a woman could become a covering to consecrate a household.

"If any woman has an unbelieving husband, and he consents to live with her, she should not leave or divorce him. For the unbelieving husband is set apart (separated, withdrawn from heathen contamination and affiliated with the Christian people) by union with his consecrated (set-apart) wife; and the unbelieving wife is set apart and separated through union with her consecrated husband. Otherwise your children would be unclean [unblessed heathen, outside the Christian covenant], but as it is they are prepared for God—pure and clean."

This doesn't say that the unbelieving husband is

saved through his wife. It just says that God can look into that household. It has become consecrated because the woman has a spiritual relationship with God. Therefore, He can answer her prayers and God can work there because the blood of Jesus is in that home to make atonement. The blood has been applied! Hallelujah!

The second point made in 1 Corinthians 11:3 is that the husband is the domestic head. Jesus is the spiritual Head. The husband is the domestic head for the family. If the husband was the spiritual head or covering, we would have to go through him to get to Jesus. And, of course, that doesn't make sense; especially if he were an unbelieving husband. If he doesn't believe, we couldn't go through him to God. There would be no fellowship with God.

First Corinthians 11 talks about the veil and the covering. I believe that this is talking about the traditional veil or scarf that the women wore over their heads in those days. In verse 16 Paul indicates that covering the head was the custom then. He also speaks about her long hair being her glory and her femininity. Referring to a man, he says that if he had long hair, it would be a shame, a dishonor, humiliating and degrading to him, speaking of a lack of masculinity. He was showing here that the woman is the glory of her husband, and that her husband has the domestic authority over her, over her body-soul realm and that she is honoring his authority over her.

There are other scriptures, too, which say that a wife should be subject to her husband. Titus 2:4 speaks about training:

"So that they will wisely train the young women to be sane and sober-minded—temperate, disciplined—and to love [their] husbands and [their] children; to be self-controlled, chaste, homemakers, good-natured (kindhearted), adapting and subordinating themselves to their husbands, that the word of God may not be exposed to reproach—

blasphemed or discredited."

"Wives, be subject to your husbands, subordinate and adapt yourselves to them—as is right and fitting and your proper duty in the Lord." (Col. 3:18).

"Wives, be subject to your husbands, as to the Lord. For the husband is the head of the wife, as Christ is the head of the church, His body, and Himself, its Saviour. As the church is subject to Christ, so let wives also be subject in everything to their husbands. However, let each one of you love his wife as himself, and let the wife see that she respects her husband" (Eph. 5:22–24,33, RSV).

We have a lot of Scripture that tells us our position, don't we? Sometimes it gets uncomfortable, especially when we don't think our husband is doing right. We shall come to that, too, when we get to the body and soul realms. Sometimes it's awfully hard. But we must learn to "plant seeds," by faith and not sight. Honor him—he will honor you, prefer him—he will prefer you, praise him—he will praise you.

Now, we have established that the wife at no time loses her direct communication with Jesus. He is still the Head of the Church. Submission is not suppression, and must never become legalistic. If it does, it becomes satanic in nature. The headship which expects submission must allow God's mercy and love to operate because submission is an *attitude* of our hearts.

If it is not in our heart to submit, we are just not going to submit. It will become a game and it won't be real, and our husband will know it! He will know it because he cannot make you submit. However, if the ideal situation exists where he is loving you and caring for you as Christ loves and cares for the church, your decision to submit will be easy and without fear.

You decide—you humble yourself, be faithful and God will surely exalt you in due time. God's Word says to do it, so the reward has to follow, for God hastens to perform His Word. If the husband is a new Christian, if he is strong and his confession is positive and if he is living a victorious life in the Word he has gained as a new Christian, then it will be easy for him to pick up and to assume this spiritual leadership. Release it to him, gently encourage him.

But, if his ego has been damaged or destroyed and he has lost his confidence in the soulish realm, then it is going to take time for him to be healed and restored. It will take the wisdom of God and spiritual intercession working through the wife to minister to these body and soul areas, until he can slip gradually into his spiritual responsibilities of leadership.

We shall be dealing with the body and soul ministry in a later chapter. Then you will see that if a woman is in a situation like this, she has hope in bringing this man on into his leadership role.

The fruit of her efforts will be the restoration of confidence in those areas where he would never stand before a group of people to give a testimony, say a closing prayer, or pray at the meal table and so forth.

Sometimes men have been so utterly destroyed that they cannot offer grace at the table, even though in their spirit they would like to. Let God use you! They need a lot of ministry, a lot of healing; they need the love and kindness and encouragement of a woman to help restore those qualities that may have been destroyed by peers or loved ones.

Chapter Six

Shall I Submit to Sin?

Is a wife, then, to submit to her husband in *everything?* This question has arisen because of certain teachings of the past few years.

Well, I say, Yes! She is to submit to him basically in all family and domestic situations. But I would say No, if he is asking her to sin. God *never* tempts or calls upon us to sin, so we should not submit to an unlawful demand of our husband. And, of course, if you read the Scripture correctly, you will see that it says to submit to him in everything "as unto the Lord," which means doing those things which line up with the rest of the Word of God.

You are not to follow him into sin. *But be sure that it IS because of SIN that you are refusing to obey, and not because of your own STUBBORN WILL. Be sure you are not saying that you don't think it is right so that you can avoid doing something that you don't care to do. Be sure that sin is the real reason why you will not do it.* Do not refuse just because you think he may be

47

making a mistake and you don't want anyone else to find out that he is not perfect! You submit—let him go ahead and make his mistake if he will. (This is not to say that you should not express your opinion. But after you have expressed your opinion, he must be free to make his decision. He is responsible for the consequences.)

Some leaders have used the example of Sarah submitting to Abraham when he told her to submit herself to the king as Abraham's sister, instead of his wife. She ended up in the king's harem.

Well, God didn't put her in this position, and God never told her to submit to this situation. Yet, because of Sarah's faith, and because God wouldn't want her to sin against her love relationship with Abraham, He delivered her out of the harem. It doesn't follow that because Sarah submitted, that is what we are supposed to do, although a lot of people have said that. It may sound ridiculous to you, but a lot of people have believed that that is exactly what we should do because of her example.

Of course, Sarah was submissive, but she was not without a voice in her family. In fact, in Genesis 21:10–12 she disagreed with Abraham, and God sided with Sarah. This shows us that we can voice our opinions, but we need to learn how to voice them properly. God always sides with *right* (see Ps. 118:6 –7)—whether it's the husband or the wife that He has to side with. Or, to put it another way: What really matters is whether we are on HIS side!

Another example of this is in 1 Samuel 25. There was Abigail, a wise woman who saved a critical situation and won the favor of David. She wasn't just a little namby-pamby woman. She actually gave good advice to David, and it was really a wonderful thing because she prevented much bloodshed.

In 1 Samuel 1:21–22 Hannah, the mother of Samuel, had a little difference with her husband. She spoke her mind and she had her way. It proved to be God's way!

So again I say, we *can* have a voice as a woman, as a wife, but we have to learn how to speak without being intimidating. And sometimes we have to let our men fail so they can grow up and succeed!

While we are on this subject, I am often asked, "Does a woman have to submit to every elder, pastor, teacher and so forth?"

I say, Yes! to the extent that we keep order in the church, and honor their authority in the body of Christ. In Ephesians 5:21 it says,

"Be subject to one another out of reverence for Christ"(RSV).

So we are to honor the gifts and the ministries that work through these people—the elders, the teachers, the pastors, whatever you want to call them—whoever stands in leadership in that portion of the body of Christ that you are in.

We are to honor them and keep order (honor the gifts and the ministries working through them). An elder or pastor does NOT have authority over your domestic affairs. They may counsel you, and they may lead you in these domestic and spiritual affairs (preferably in the company of your husband), but they are to lead you, and not to drive you.

We have many problems of this nature in the charismatic movement today. There are some so-called shepherds, pastors, elders or what-have-you who are actually ruling people's lives—they are ruling homes, domestic situations, rather than counseling and guiding—and they are bringing people into bondage!

They are not your spiritual head. Jesus is *still* the spiritual Head of the church. Praise God! He is the One to whom we ultimately submit. He is the One from whom we get direction. Sometimes He works through a husband, an elder, a pastor or friend in guidance. But it is wonderful to know that we *do* have that special

49

relationship with Jesus: that as a woman (or wife) we can go directly to Him in the Spirit and have our needs met.

PART TWO

Our Ministry in the Soul

Chapter Seven

The Battle Within

There are spiritual principles we need to understand about the human soul before we can start applying natural laws and principles.

If we understand the function of our own soul, then how much better will we understand the functioning of our husband's soul, our children's souls and all those around us. In understanding the soul's function we then can minister life, restoration and growth to those we love.

Remember, we are triune persons with triune needs. As a wife we are learning to minister to our husband's needs— our spirit to his spirit— our soul to his soul— our body to his body.

Let's take a look again at our chart on page 20. We have the body, which consists of the five senses—our flesh, blood and bones. Through this body everything that happens in our spirit and soul areas is manifested. We have the spirit man, which is called the "hidden man of the heart" or conscience. This is where we have fellowship and relationship with God our Father. Then we have the soul, which consists of the intellect, attitudes, emotions and will.

We have in this realm of the soul, (or mind) a battleground where we can receive either *good* or *evil* thoughts. GOOD thoughts come into our mind from the Holy Spirit or from intellectual knowledge coming into or stored in our mind (good thoughts, of course, would have to line up with the Word of God). These GOOD thoughts placed in our mind, examined and computed by our spirit (conscience), come out of us at our will in a positive response of faith, power and good fruits.

Our soul (mind) can also receive lies from Satan, through the lusts of the flesh and an unrenewed mind. Evil thoughts can come into our mind (our heart, See Acts 5:1– 4; John 13:2). All of the thoughts in our mind must be sorted out. We keep the good and discard the bad. If we allow the lies of Satan to find a place in us, and we fellowship with them, they will emerge as doubt and unbelief, and cause us to have negative responses. Later we shall discuss the negative responses of our bodies, but now we are examining what happens in the soul realm if we act, react and think wrongly.

The object, then, is to make the soul realm subject to our spirit, with the power of the Holy Spirit flowing through us. We know that our spirit, the born-again spirit, cannot have control over the soul unless our WILL is submitted to God. We still have to make the decision to yield even though we have a born-again spirit. We still have a mind, a free will. We are still "free-will agents." We have to submit our will to God for our spirit to gain control over our soul.

Then the mind, the intellect, can be renewed by reading and hearing the Word, being washed, made clean and restored to right thinking by it. In consequence, our desires, our reactions, our attitudes and our emotions become right desires, right reactions, right attitudes and right emotions. The Word says,

"Roll your works upon the Lord—commit and trust them wholly to Him; [He will cause your thoughts to become agreeable to His will, and] so shall your plans be established and succeed" (Prov. 16:3).

Yes, your very thoughts will agree with God's will when you decide to commit and trust ALL things to Him.

In chapter two, we touched on the subject of the unrenewed mind. I want to refer to this again because this is part of our soul realm. This is the groundwork that we are going to have to lay before we can help ourselves (receive God's help to come out of our marital problems and other hang-ups we may have). You remember I said an *unrenewed* mind will produce unforgiveness, fear, hate, jealousy, self-pity, lonesomeness, rebellion, resentment, selfishness, strife, unbelief, self-righteousness and doubt. All of these are classified as **"works of the flesh"** in Galatians 5:19–21.

They come from the lust of the flesh. They come from the world. They don't come from the Spirit of God, they come from the other spirit—from the enemy, the devil. On the other hand, the renewed mind is operating in that soul which has the mind of Christ (see 1 Cor. 1:30). Because we have Christ in us, the Bible says that we have the wisdom of God. He can operate through our mind because we have a born-again spirit which, in conjunction with the Holy Spirit, can take control of our soul realm, and therefore impart to us the wisdom of Christ.

With our soul subject to our born-again spirit, we become transmitters of the fruit of the Spirit. Galatians 5:22–23 says,

"But the fruit of the (Holy) Spirit, [the work which His presence within accomplishes]—is love, joy (gladness), peace, patience (an even temper, forbearance), kindness, goodness (benevolence), faithfulness; (meekness, humility) gentleness, self-control (self-restraint, continence)..."

In a renewed mind, then, we do have faith! We believe! We have power! We remember also that this spiritual fruit is GROWN, not acquired. We have to develop such fruit through our renewed mind. We don't just all of a sudden (because of our spirit becoming born again), have a renewed mind so that the fruit starts blossoming right out of our mouth. This is not the case. We have to be fed by the Word and let the Holy Spirit activate our spirit to the renewing of our mind, and so bring forth these "fruits." Thus, they will grow and be manifested.

Chapter Eight

Our Helper

In Romans 12:2, we read, **"Do not be conformed to this world—this age, fashioned after and adapted to its external, superficial customs. But be transformed (changed) by the [entire] renewal of your mind—by its new ideals and its new attitude—so that you may prove [for yourselves] what is the good and acceptable and perfect will of God even the thing which is good and acceptable and perfect [in His sight for you]."**

Do not be conformed to the idea of the world that if your marriage isn't working and you don't "feel" happy, you just divorce and try again with someone else. NO, Christian "Babe," hang in there and use the power of the Holy Spirit to get your soul and your husband's soul on the side of God.

If we have been on the side of the world for quite a while, it will take the power of the Word of God to renew our mind. Just as in a marriage which is "on the rocks," it requires dealing with EVERY attitude and emotion, as well as the will of the wife and the husband for the HEALING power of the Holy Spirit to do His work. Sometimes this takes longer than we like, but it is the grace of God showing us "self " little by little. Most of us would be too discouraged if we saw all at once the work that had to be done.

The power of the Holy Spirit becomes effective in us when we receive the baptism of the Holy Spirit with the evidence of speaking in tongues (see Acts 1:8). Our spiritual language is of the utmost importance in our Christian walk. I would like to share some scriptures that will help you in this.

In Romans 8:26 –27,

"Likewise the Spirit helps us in our weakness; for we do not know how to pray as we ought, but the Spirit Himself intercedes for us with sighs too deep for words. And he who searches the hearts of men knows what is the mind of the Spirit, because the Spirit intercedes for the saints according to the will of God." (RSV)

This says plainly that the Holy Spirit helps us in our weakness, marital problems, unrenewed mind, sick body and so forth. We all have weaknesses. We aren't perfect yet, but the Holy Spirit knows how to pray when He comes into us. He "marries" our spirit, as it were. When that marriage or merger takes place, the Holy Spirit and your spirit become one and produce a heavenly language that makes intercession for the saints, yourself and your family, and the Spirit glorifies and praises our Father.

In 1 Corinthians 14:2 we read,

"For one who speaks in an [unknown] tongue speaks not to men but to God, for no one understands or catches his meaning, because in the (Holy) Spirit he utters secret truths and hidden things [not obvious to the understanding]."

This tells us that God understands you. You may not understand the language that is coming out of your mouth. Even expert linguists might have no comprehension of these languages. However, we have experienced times when the tongue spoken was a language of *man*, an unusual circumstance used as a specific witness.

Speaking in tongues, sometimes called our spiritual language, has nothing to do with your mind. We speak to God by our spirit and the Holy Spirit, and God understands. In this way, He hears and does meet our needs, even when we don't know what those deep-seated needs in our lives really are.

In the fourth verse of the same chapter, Paul says, **"He who speaks in a tongue edifies himself."** Whom does he edify? He edifies *himself.* This is important to grasp. If you want to be edified, you MUST get this soul under control. You MUST allow the spirit to begin controlling the soul. This takes place in the realm of your mind, your intellect.

In the thirteenth verse of that same chapter it says,

"Therefore, he who speaks in a tongue should pray for the power to interpret "(RSV).

That is the answer to the ones who say, "Well, if I can't understand the language that comes out of my mouth, how in the world will I ever become edified? How could it ever change me if I don't understand what I'm saying?" The fourteenth and fifteenth verses say,

"For if I pray in a tongue, my spirit prays but my mind is unfruitful. What am I to do? I will pray with the spirit and I will pray with the mind also; (my soul realm) **I will sing with the spirit and I will sing with the mind also"** (RSV, parentheses mine).

This is how the mind becomes edified. It never says that the mind understands word-for-word what this language is that is coming out of your mouth. It is not a translation, but the Word says here that we are to pray for the power to interpret. An interpretation is just the "gist" of something, isn't it? It's not a word-for-word translation. These verses tell us that as you pray in the

Spirit in your spiritual language, your mind will become edified because you are going to pray to interpret this language that comes out of your mouth.

You will praise God and pray according to what the Holy Spirit is praying. You will pray also in English (if this is your native language). Therefore, your mind will become edified, and as you are doing this and learning, you may only get a few words in your native language, but there will be enough that the Holy Spirit will let you know the way this language is going. It may be all praise and thanksgiving to the Father. It may also confirm God's direction for your life and bring exhortation and comfort.

It is sheer joy when you find you can lift your voice in praise, in spiritual song, to the tune of your vacuum, clothes dryer or mixmaster—taking care of natural responsibilities and at the same time worshiping, making intercession and **"building up yourselves on your most holy faith, praying in the Holy Spirit"** (Jude 20, KJV).

"Praying in the Holy Spirit." Now, that's not your mind praying. This is how many of us have prayed for many years—just with our mind, in English, because that is all that we understood. We didn't know about being filled with the Holy Spirit and speaking in tongues.

We're admonished to pray in the Holy Spirit. For what purpose? To build yourself up, building your mind up, your soul. With the power of the Holy Spirit working in us, we reach the place where we can get our spirit to take authority over our soul and bring it under subjection.

Tongues can also be intercession not only for your needs, but also for the needs of your family. It is really vital as a wife and as a mother that we have this power. The gift of the Holy Spirit is for everyone. The Bible says that we should repent, be baptized and receive the gift of the Holy Ghost (see Acts 2:38). Repentance is the only requirement in the Bible for receiving the Holy Spirit. It is a change of your views, the acceptance of God's will into your life and receiving forgiveness of sins in the name of Jesus Christ.

There is not one born-again Christian that should go on without receiving this power. After all, Jesus told the disciples who had walked with Him and talked with Him day after day for at least three years that although they had witnessed miracles and so forth they needed the power of the Holy Spirit. Without Him (the third Person), they couldn't live a Christian life. Peter denied Christ three times, yet he had seen Him do miracles and he knew He was the Son of God. He had confessed to Jesus' face that He was the Son of God, and yet he didn't have the power and the strength within himself to walk out the Christian life. And so, because He knew it, Jesus told them, "Wait here until you receive the Holy Spirit."

There they were, waiting, as it is told in the first part of the book of Acts, and the Holy Spirit fell and 120 people received the baptism of the Holy Spirit, including Jesus' mother and all the women who were serving the disciples. As wives, women and mothers our lives are touched by many people—all the members of our family depend on us so much—there are schedules and all kinds of demands to be met—we can't truly meet these needs in the natural. We must have the supernatural power of God to help us.

This means, then, that you are not depending on your husband. You are not depending on your boyfriend, nor are you depending on your pastor or even your friends. You are not depending on anyone except *you*. Just you alone—you and your fellowship with God by the Holy Spirit for the edification of yourself, your mind, your soul and then for the needs of your loved ones.

When we depend on our *personal* relationship with our heavenly Father to meet our needs then we will *never* be disappointed. His love *never* fails! Many times our brothers or sisters, sons or daughters, husbands or best friends fail us because they aren't perfected yet and we're disappointed, sometimes to despair. Get your eyes and your mind back on your Lord and He will surely keep you in perfect peace, meeting every need.

"You will guard him and keep him in perfect and constant peace whose mind [both its inclination and its character] is stayed on You, because he commits himself to You, leans on You and hopes confidently in You" (Isa. 26:3).

Chapter Nine

Interpersonal Relationship

W hat would you say is a wife's greatest need in the marriage relationship? Yes, you're right, it's to be loved and to know that her husband believes that she is a gift from God. Those of you who are married, can you say that you really know in your heart that your husband believes that you are a gift from God?

In Proverbs 18:22 Solomon says,

"He who finds a [true] wife finds a good thing!"

The question is, are you? **"And obtains favor of the Lord."** Praise God! My husband finally believes that he has a good thing in me! In fact the day he admitted that I was his greatest earthly asset was to me a day of victory. I knew then that at last the many changes I had had to make were really appreciated by him.

How can we make ourselves lovable, then? We all have a need to be loved. I know me; if my husband doesn't tell me he loves me, I just don't feel good! I don't feel right. Not only do I have to FEEL that he loves me; I need to hear him SAY he loves me. There were many years in our marriage, before we knew Jesus, that I begged, squalled and bawled and tried every way that I knew to get him to *say* "I love you!" Finally he would say it because I had nagged it out of him, but it wasn't by his free will. It wasn't what I wanted, so it never satisfied. It was just another nagging situation, with a grudging response to keep me quiet.

We need to MAKE ourselves lovable, so that he will say, "I love you!" and we know it hasn't been worked up. The FIRST thing we have to do is to establish the principle that we must live to follow Jesus and seek His righteousness first because *nothing will work without Jesus*—not a thing! We also have to find out we are the righteousness of God in Christ Jesus (see 2 Cor. 5:21). Even though we are not perfect in every area, we can still say that we are the righteousness of God—working out His principles in our life.

SECONDLY, be honest! Being honest with yourself and with God takes a lot of courage. It did for me, and it still does. THIRDLY, be willing to change. Humble yourself and God will exalt you. That's scriptural, isn't it? And in saying this, we are saying: "Be willing to change, even though he should be the one that should change the most in some particular area." You be the one to humble yourself and change, or keep a good attitude and in so doing, leave the door open wide for him.

You will be surprised how wide the door is opened when you humble yourself. I know this is one thing that helped to heal our relationship so fast from the effects of fifteen years of marriage without Jesus, when my husband humbled himself to me. I know it works, not because I did it, but because he did it first, and I saw the principle work.

He would come to me sometimes when I was entirely at fault and would say, "I'm sorry! I'm sorry I did this or said that!" I KNEW it was my fault. It made me feel so ashamed of myself, but it helped me come back into a proper relationship with him. The door was open—he was accepting me faults and all. It made it very easy for me to say, "Oh no, it was really my fault. I shouldn't have done that!" And before I knew it, I was exalting him. The Word worked!

This is the kind of humbling we are talking about, submitting to each other in love. Your husband will exalt you, too, just as my husband has exalted me when I have said that I was sorry. You see, I have taken the same place too. So I know it works.

When you fail, first forgive yourself after asking God to forgive you, and be determined to TRY AGAIN. There are many habit patterns that we have formed through our "old" nature. Attitudes, emotions and reactions learned from our mothers, our aunts or others were instrumental in influencing our formative years. We may have just picked up these attitudes anywhere; from movies, television or even from fairy tales. It is surprising how many little girls still dream about Cinderella and want this kind of life even after they grow up. There is nothing wrong with that; we can have that, you know. It need not be fantasy. We can make it become real. Little girls and big girls hold onto the Cinderella ideas because really this is a right idea—the many principles of a "Prince Charming" taking care of her are in God's plan for women.

Self-acceptance, then, is an important thing as well as our forgiving others. If we hold unforgiveness in our hearts, it's a terrible thing and it will stop the fruit of the Spirit from being manifested in our lives, as well as keep our minds from being renewed. So forgiveness of self and others will help bring deliverance from the fruit-deeds of the flesh.

Chapter Ten

Keep the Door Open

God loves us—so much that continuously He leaves the "Chamber Door" open to us through Christ. We always have an avenue to our Father. Jesus has already opened the door, and if we walk through by Jesus, we are there. The secret to God's forgiveness is our confession to Him of our sins, and the repentance of them. Knowing by the Word of God they are forgiven, we receive forgiveness.

Some of us have had an unrenewed mind so long, not understanding forgiveness, that the devil is free to intimidate us and bring us into condemnation. Here, I will lay a firm foundation for forgiveness from the Scriptures.

"As far as the east is from the west, so far has He removed our transgressions from us" (Ps. 103:12).

How far is the east from the west? They never meet, do they? That is how far God has removed confessed sin from you and from HIM. He doesn't ever see it. It is removed from Him. The Word says,

"So far does He remove our transgressions from us.

"He will again have compassion upon us. He will subdue and tread underfoot our iniquities. You will cast all our sins into the depths of the sea" (Mic. 7:19).

He puts them into the deepest part of the sea, never to be remembered again. He puts a big "NO FISHING" sign there for the devil. Therefore, do not allow the devil to take you back to the old memories that God has buried. They are gone!

" I, even I, am He who blots out and cancels your transgressions for My own sake, and I will not remember your sins" (Isa. 43:25).

See, God has no memory of confessed sins. He says in that scripture, "For My own sake!" Not just for your sake does he remove the sins, but they have to be removed for His own sake because He WANTS fellowship with you. It's not just that you want it and you need it. He needs you; He wants you! He wants your sins to be removed and blotted out, so that He can come to you and show His love to you.

In Jeremiah 31:34 God says,

"...I will forgive their iniquity, and I will (seriously) remember their sin no more."

NO MORE! "I WILL FORGIVE," God repeated this in Hebrews 8:12. It is God's will to forgive. The entire Bible talks about God reaching out to His people. Anyone, ANYONE, who will reach out toward God through Jesus Christ will find God reach out toward them. It is His will to forgive.

"So repent—change your mind and purpose; turn around and return [to God], that your sins may be erased (blotted out, wiped clean), that times of refreshing—of recovering from the effects of heat, of reviving with fresh air—may come from the presence of the Lord" (Acts 3:19).

That is where He wants us to be. He wants our sins

to be blotted out, and they are! Then we come into times of refreshing in the presence of the Lord, where He builds us up and restores everything that the devil tried to tear down and destroy.

"Come now, and let us reason together, says the Lord; though your sins be as scarlet, they shall be as white as snow; though they be red like crimson, they shall be as wool" (Isa. 1:18).

God makes you clean, clean, CLEAN! Pure! WHITE! Isn't that marvelous? It's all gone! All that sin is blotted away. Praise the Lord!

"For by a single offering He has forever completely cleansed and perfected those who are consecrated and made holy. And also the Holy Spirit adds His testimony to us [in confirmation of this]. For having said, this is the agreement (testament, covenant) that I will set up and conclude with them after those days, says the Lord: I will imprint My laws upon their hearts, and I will inscribe them on their minds—on their inmost thoughts and understanding, He then goes on to say, And their sins and their lawbreakings I will remember no more. Now where there is absolute remission—forgiveness and cancellation of the penalty—of these [sins and lawbreakings] there is no longer any offering made to atone for sin" (Heb. 10:14–18).

Hallelujah! We don't need any more offerings or sacrifices!

Once there is forgiveness, there is no need to EVER bring it up again.

"Therefore, brethren, since we have full freedom and confidence to enter into the [Holy of] Holies [by the power and virtue] in the blood of Jesus, by this fresh (new) and living way which He initiated and dedicated and opened for us through the separating curtain [veil of the Holy of Holies] that is, through His flesh; and since we have [such] a great and wonderful and noble Priest [Who rules] over the

house of God, let us all come forward and draw near with true (honest and sincere) hearts in unqualified assurance and absolute conviction engendered by faith, [that is, by that leaning of the entire human personality on God in absolute trust and confidence in His power, wisdom and goodness], having our hearts sprinkled and purified from a guilty (evil) conscience and with our bodies cleansed with pure water.

So let us seize and hold fast and retain without wavering the hope we cherish and confess, and our acknowledgment of it, for He Who promised is reliable (sure) and faithful to His word" (Heb. 10:19–23).

Glory, hallelujah! We are in the Presence of God. We are His. We belong to Him. This is where we are going to stay.

If you make a little mistake, don't be afraid and get condemned, and run farther away from the Father into darkness. Always run back to the Father and say, "Forgive me!" Walk in the light as He is in the light, and He will help you. He knows that you can't do it all at once, especially if you are just coming into your walk with the Lord. You may stumble around a little bit, but He is going to be right there to pick you up if you are willing to say, "Father, I goofed! Help me, forgive me!" He loves that. How much do you love it, even as a mother, when your child comes to you and says, "Oh, Mommy, I'm sorry." You just want to gather him up in your arms and cover him with love. That's how God feels.

Don't ever let the devil try to rob you! If he brings back to your mind memories of the past sins you have committed, don't receive them. They are forgiven. If you need to, get out this list of scriptures we have quoted and just read them off to him. Tell him where your sins are—as far as the east is from the west, gone into the depths of the ocean. They are gone and God has forgotten them. Tell Satan, "You are a liar and a deceiver, and you have no right to bring them up again!"

You may have to put a date on it. I once had to do this because I had a terrible bout with resentment, and the devil knew exactly the right memory to bring back to my mind. He knew it hurt my heart worse than anything that had happened in our marriage. He knew that if I would fellowship with that thought, he would have me back again and the resentment would come back into my heart.

Finally I had to say, "Devil, as of February 1970, I forgave my husband for that particular thing, and you have no right to bring it back to my mind, EVER!" My husband joined me in prayer and we cast away that spirit which had tried to bring me back into the prison of resentment.

Previous to that we had learned to confess these sins to each other, especially when we each knew the other was *already aware* of those particular sins. And when we asked each other's forgiveness, and the Lord's, the way was open to heal, to release bitterness, resentment, fear, jealousy and so forth.

Please note that I said here that we confessed sins that *each* of us was already aware of. We don't think it is necessary to bring up old sins which we know the other person knows nothing about, adding grief and hurt feelings to our mate unnecessarily. If you confess *these* things to God and have repented, it is best to leave them *there*, never to be remembered again by you or God.

Just as it is important for us to keep the doorway open to God's love, it is also important to keep the doorway open to your husband's love. Openly forgive him and forget it!

"And whenever you stand praying, if you have anything against any one, forgive him and let it drop—leave it, let it go—in order that your Father Who is in heaven may also forgive you your [own] failings and shortcomings and let them drop" (Mark 11:25).

Chapter Eleven

Perfectionism

There are many ways that we try to be *good* wives — by having an immaculate house, clean clothes, clean car, clean yard, being a good cook, super manager of the household and so forth. However, when these duties are performed to the point of perfectionism, we very often find that they stem from pride to create our image—OUR image in OUR house.

These ways of being a good wife are all good and needed. It is good to have a clean house, and it is good to have clean children, and it is good to have a clean yard, but it is not good if our image is depending on these things. The woman who is depending on these things for recognition to prove what a "good wife" she is, is the woman who has the tendency to be running everything. Everything must be controlled by her because her image is at stake. The results are that she becomes physically worn out and driven by perfectionism: "Take off your shoes!" "Don't walk on that shiny floor, I just waxed it!" "Be careful when you wash your hands in the bathroom. Don't leave any water marks on the faucet!" She has no time to *listen* to her husband or children to minister to their spiritual and soulish needs. She is just too busy "running" and trying to perfect her image.

She becomes a fault-finder because she is a perfectionist. She finds fault with everybody and everything. She opens herself to that dominating spirit which usurps authority from her husband and grabs for his responsibilities. Now she is in big trouble. She really thinks she is something. She becomes *Independent, Capable* and *Efficient.* Behold, the ICE woman cometh! (see chapter 2.)

Two direct results of perfectionism are self-righteousness and deceitfulness. Have you ever seen a woman who has a "home face"? When she is busy at home she wears a "home face," but when she is out with her friends, she puts on her "friend face." All the way home from church she wears a "judge face," tight-lipped and frowning. She told her children and husband all the way to church just what they should and shouldn't have done and by the time they reached the church everyone was upset. In disbelief we see her walking in the door, beaming, "Oh sister so-and-so, praise God! Isn't it a beautiful day?" Deceitful woman.

Wouldn't it be great if she would determine in her heart to put on that "happy face" for her family, just like she does for her friends. It's a matter of WILL, because we don't always FEEL like it.

A wife who is caught up in perfectionism, making her "perfect wife" image, often tries to remake her husband, trying to conform him to the image that *she* wants in *her* house.

Having gone through the bout with perfectionism myself, I suddenly, by the grace of God, saw myself and desired to make a change in my attitudes and the expectations of those around me. When the big change occurred in me, I received flowers every week. My husband was so excited that I had finally gotten rid of this perfectionist garbage and realized that I really wanted to be a good wife for him and not an "image" for myself, it was hard for him to believe that I was the same woman! I had always dreamed of my husband bringing me flowers (another Cinderella dream), and when he started bringing them, it was joy unspeakable.

Right then the devil came and said to me, "Well, the only reason he is bringing them is that there is something going on..." But we had been far enough down the road that I knew there wasn't anything "going on." I knew that he loved me and was really appreciating the NEW me. He still brings flowers and dozens of other gifts from time to time, which far exceed any of my expectations. The blessings and side benefits of having right attitudes and fulfilling our role correctly can overtake us!

I know many of us (including me) would be happy if hubby came in the front door, having picked a dandelion off the front yard, and said, "Here honey, I love you!" It isn't the flowers that matter, it is the thought behind them that is so precious. It is a special way of saying, "I love you!" We as women need and appreciate these outward signs of love. Remember, if he at one time showed these outward signs and stopped, you can *learn* how to have them back and have a happier husband.

What about your husband—what does he need? What is his greatest need in your marriage? How does he feel? Your man needs to be accepted and admired by you. These are the two vital soul needs he has. He wants and needs to be loved, just as you need his love, but this need for acceptance and admiration that *you* can give him can be the key to his successes and the encouragement he needs to overcome past failure, inferiorities and the pressures of the world—and even more it can cause him to appreciate you.

Ephesians 5:33 speaks this principle of acceptance and admiration loud and clear.

"However, let each man of you (without exception) love his wife as [being in a sense] his very own self; and let the wife see that she respects and reverences her husband—that she notices him, regards him, honors him, prefers him, venerates and esteems him; and that she defers to him, praises him, and loves and admires him exceedingly."

I heard a famous man say that there were three things that he felt he needed in his personal life. One of them was to be desired and respected by a godly woman. That comes out of admiration and acceptance doesn't it? That same need has to be fulfilled in every man no matter who he is: Billy Graham, Bill Basansky, the president of the United States or the Sheik of Arabia. Whoever he is, his greatest need (next to Christ) is to be admired and accepted by his woman.

Acceptance and admiration come from our soul to meet his soul need. This isn't just our own natural ability. Remember our spirit by the Holy Spirit power influences our soul to minister *life* to our husbands.

If we are not accepting our husband as he is, but are in fact trying to change him, we can actually destroy love. We can destroy that first love! Remember when you were dating and then first married, how sweet it was? Well, this excitement and joy of the "first love" is the first thing that comes into jeopardy and is the very thing that we want to keep alive. As Christian married women we realize that marriage is until "death do us part," so why shouldn't we continue to "receive flowers" and *continue* to experience the excitement of our "first love" relationship.

Usually the only thing that stands in our way is *self*. When I first started seeking to improve our marriage relationship, I ran across this true story which I would like to share with you.

The man of our story was an internationally famous writer who married a beautiful woman. He told how much in love he and his wife were when they first married. They were so much in love and he was so enthralled about their relationship that he wrote diaries filled with descriptions of it. He told of her attitudes and their ways together—everything was just so beautiful.

He wrote poetry about their love and, as time went by, he became more famous than ever and very rich. Yet, he still didn't feel fulfilled as a man, and so he started looking for something else. After he studied the teachings of Jesus and other teachers of good morals, as a personal conviction he felt that he should give most of his worldly possessions away and he did. His wife was disagreeing, screaming and kicking all the way. As he was starting to sell the publishing rights to all of his literary works, his wife threw a fit. She told him that if he went ahead and fulfilled his plans, she would kill herself. She went on and on because she didn't want him to destroy the material life of riches that they had together. Yet, it was in the heart of this man to change his life. He wanted a quieter, more simple life.

She stayed with him, but very grudgingly. They moved out to a little cottage in the woods where he chopped his own wood and made his own shoes. It was really a wonderful life, he thought. They had all of their needs met.

Because they weren't living in the lap of luxury as they had been, she hated it! She degraded him. She did everything she could do to discourage this dear man. Forty-eight years of marriage went by, and we find them as a very old couple. She is on her knees, begging him to read aloud some of the beautiful poetry that he had written about their "first love." As he read they both cried bitter tears. With her words, attitudes and emotions, she had destroyed the inside of her man and their beautiful love.

The story goes on to say that when he was on his deathbed, his dying request was that she not be allowed to see him. He died without her seeing him and now, when it was too late, she realized what she had done.

She had killed the one thing that meant the most to her—his love.

Well, that's a pretty extreme story, but I guess sometimes it takes something like that for the Lord to show some people where they have missed it. That is the story the Lord used to show me I had destroyed the "first love" in our marriage. And you know, when I saw it, it was a pretty bad shock. I spent a few hours in the bedroom actually so grieved in my spirit that I was nearly physically ill. My husband came to me and I confessed my shortcomings amid buckets of tears, and we prayed about it. We talked it over, and he told me how he knew that most of these things were on account of sins we had already confessed to each other and were forgiven. But I then explained to him how I was willing to change because I could see how I had destroyed our first love.

I had to come to that point in myself where I saw in myself what I had done with my mouth, with my actions and with my reactions that had slowly degenerated the first fifteen years of our marriage. It was a slow thing, like a cancer that ate at our marriage and ate at our love. We merely existed together...until Jesus came! Jesus restored it all as we submitted our WILLS to Him to change and it's a happy ending. Praise God!

As I spent more hours on my knees, the Holy Spirit showed me that I had not realized that I have a soul and body ministry to my man. I had thought surely, since we were both born again and filled with the Holy Spirit, that will solve everything. We had a good spiritual togetherness, but what a relief it was to discover how I could minister life and restoration to our soulish relationship.

Jesus said, "Humble yourself and I will exalt you." It's true, His Word works!

Chapter Twelve

The Good Confession

We have often heard that behind every successful man is a "good" wife, and it is true. A wife who can accept her husband just like he is—like they say, "can *make* him" or without acceptance "*break* him."

Trying to change a man can cause severe marriage problems. It can cause his attitudes to change toward you, and your attitudes and reactions to change toward him. These attitudes may start changing in the living room, but they can become bedroom problems. Trying to totally possess and conform a man to your idea of what he should be like can cause your man to rebel.

This doesn't mean that you can never discuss good or bad attitudes, goals, dreams and so forth with your husband, but it does mean that it is very important for you to have the right attitude and the fruit of the Spirit working through you when you are having these serious discussions. Certainly it would be well for us to be far removed from our feminine emotions in times of serious discussions, as these emotions oftentimes override what our spirit is transmitting to our soul and what should be coming out of our mouths as sensible and wise counsel.

The bottom line is: it doesn't work! You can't change your man. YOU can't, but the HOLY SPIRIT CAN! So we must show him that we accept him just as he is. We have trouble in this area as women because we don't want him to make any mistakes, and we don't want anyone to know he isn't perfect! That's why we have a tendency to say, "Oh honey, if you would just do this and this." Or, "Oh, be careful and don't do that because such-and-such might happen!" We are always so quick, instead of letting them go ahead and make the mistake. Maybe you have already told him once; don't tell him again. Let him go ahead and do it. Let him make the mistake. Most of the time this is the only way he will change and mature if need be.

Accepting him means *not* to try to change him. The woman who does this usually comes across as a self-righteous woman, although she may not mean to. So if you find yourself trying to change him, check *yourself* for the soulish fault of self-righteousness. Don't look at his faults. If you find yourself in this area of finding faults, check yourself for self-centeredness.

A man, no matter how many faults he has, has some good points. It is up to you to discover them, even if it is nothing more than just the way he combs his hair. Talk it up! Love him for it! Compliment him for it! You would be surprised what will come of it. I realize this is a trivial point to start on (the way he combs his hair), but often I talk to women who are so discouraged and disappointed that this is about the only good thing they can think of for starters!

Never talk negatively about your husband to anyone. Now this does not eliminate counseling. If you have a problem, and you need to go to someone who will help you handle it in the Spirit, with the help of the Lord, it's OK. But don't go around to every sister Sally, telling her all the bad things about your husband; don't even tell her one little thing. It isn't any of her business. You are to protect your husband. He is yours!

"Death and life are in the power of the tongue, and they who indulge it shall eat the fruit of it [for death or life]" (Prov. 18:21).

If you talk negatively about your man, you are going to start believing it. If you start mouthing his faults, you are giving life to them, and they will become *bigger and stronger* strongholds of division for the enemy to use. And he *will* use them. He wants you to make mountains out of molehills because it makes it easier for him to drive a wedge into your marriage.

It's up to you to start confessing (out loud to him), giving voice to all the good things about him; his good side: "Honey, you are a good provider. I really appreciate the way that you provide for us. The bills are always paid."

Maybe you don't have "lots and lots" of everything, but at least the tax collector and the credit company are not on your front doorstep! There are a lot of compliments to give a man who just keeps things even with the board—maybe you don't have anything left over at the end of the month, but if he is making ends meet, he is to be complimented.

After you compliment him, chances are that he may try even harder to have more left over at the end of the next month. If he is dependable or if he is honest, praise him. Honesty can come from a man who may have a thousand other faults, but you can voice to him how much you appreciate him being an honest man. These words of "life" express confidence in him.

We fail so often in this area. We are very quick to tell him his faults, but we are very slow to show him his positive, good side. Don't let him know his faults get on your nerves. This is a very hard thing to do when these faults are embarrassing events for us. But I know that you and the Lord can figure out how to get around whatever it is that really bothers you. Pray about it and the Lord will show you. I know it's hard to not let your husband know what is going on in your stomach, but you also need to realize that many of his faults that are irritating you are entirely unintentional on his part.

Another thing I would say is, DON'T NAG. Do you know what nagging is? It's saying something *more* than *once*!

"It is better to live in the corner of an attic than with a crabby woman in a lovely home" (Prov. 21:9, TLB).

"A constant dripping on a rainy day and a cranky woman are much alike! You can no more stop her complaints than you can stop the wind or hold onto anything with oil-slick hands" (Prov. 27:15, TLB).

"A rebellious son is a calamity to his father and a nagging wife annoys like constant dripping" (Prov. 19:13, TLB).

Don't ever compare your man with another man. Every man is different. Every man has a different purpose and a different personality. It can really hurt him to be compared with another man. It hurts his male ego.

Don't give him books to read to help him self-improve! A lot of women who have unsaved husbands have done this. You know they leave printed tracts on the toilet, a Bible lying open by the bed, things underlined in a book lying open by his favorite chair. They do all of these little tricks to try to get him to change, to improve. These methods seldom work, usually causing him to feel intimidated. A real change in your attitude and reactions is far more effective.

Accept his purpose in life as your purpose also. Become one in purpose just as God the Father, God the Son and God the Holy Spirit are one. They are a *triune* Being. They have *one* purpose. They work together. That's the way we should be with our husbands. We should come together in spirit, soul and body. We are triune beings also. We have to come together in all three areas to keep things in balance, to make each one of us a whole person. We come together with him, become *one* in the soul, and therefore an extension of his purpose.

I think one of the women I could use as a perfect example of this is Evelyn Roberts (the wife of Oral Roberts). I realize she isn't perfect (I don't know anyone who is *perfect*, but I think she is pretty close to it). I've been with her enough to know how she feels about her husband. I know that she is a loving and submissive wife. I know she has made herself an extension of him in every way. She is an extension of his purpose at Oral Roberts University and the Oral Roberts Association, an extension of everything that he stands for...not only in God, but in their home. In all of that she has not lost her own "identity" (as the world would say). For several years she was a successful schoolteacher and soon the mother of four children. She has written books, and currently speaks for ladies' groups, civic groups, conventions, television interviews and so forth. She keeps herself well informed and yet, with all these activities, she has kept a consistent, successful marriage relationship. She stays submissive to him in love, and in agreement with their purpose as ONE.

UNITY DOES NOT MEAN UNIFORMITY!

There are many marriages in which the husband is a perfectionist and the wife is the exact opposite (or vice versa). This difference sometimes causes a lot of problems. His mother taught him to have everything "just so," and to him, if anything is left out of order and isn't "just so," he thinks of her as a bad housekeeper. It is easy to see that these kinds of attitudes and expectations are due to the way we were raised by our parents. However, the Holy Spirit can help us work out these areas in our lives, bringing balance within us, not only in the natural, but also in the supernatural. We become the strength in their weakness, and they become the strength in our weakness. It balances out as we become an extension of each other. It's really super when we get to this place of seeing the balance and helping each other.

There is a spirit in the world that says a woman HAS to take HER place in this world and she HAS to have HER identity. Through the lust of the flesh many are being deceived.

As a Christian, first and foremost, our identity is in Christ our Savior, whether we are single or married. No person can have true inner peace and know WHO they are without the inner confidence that through Jesus we can "have" all things which pertain to life and godliness and "be" all things to all people. We are seldom told that we *can* have, and as a married person, we *should* have the attitude of becoming an extension of someone else. Why are our young couples having to learn so much in their marriages? It is because we have had few people bold enough to tell us or to show us that you can walk in corporate purpose and be an extension of your mate, and you *don't lose* your identity by doing so.

To have unity of purpose, we have to be united with our mate. You, as a wife, must say, "I really want to become one with you in this purpose in your life (as a businessman, laborer, doctor, teacher, lawyer or whatever he is doing). I can see that God wants to use you in this capacity, and I want to get behind you 100 percent. I want to help you in this. I want to be part of it with you in thought, word, deed and prayer." How could he turn down such an attitude? That is humility and God will exalt you because you are humbling yourself to come to him and say, "Man, I missed it! Help me to be 'one' with you in your purpose. I see how I have pulled away from you."

Again, this does not mean that you have lost your opportunity to be successfully creative. However, if you do work outside your home, the importance of *his* job should have priority.

Do you have a problem with self-centeredness? It could have been brought on by this idea of having to find your own identity. To change, you can start by doing SPECIAL things for your husband, your children or your friends. In looking at the lives of those around you, there is always someone who needs you. A word of caution: in extending help outside your home do not let it be at the expense of your relationships at home. This is a very important thing to remember. Some women get a little *carried away* helping outside their homes and they are the losers when it is done to such an extent that the husband and/or children are neglected. If you ever wanted to solve a world problem, this would be the time to do it. Think about it. When society doesn't have to end up supporting and rehabilitating your husband and children, then you have been instrumental in solving a world problem! If you have the drive that you MUST get out and help society, remember, *you are helping society right in your home. You can be instrumental in making your husband and children successful, productive, happy people!* It takes a lot of work, coordinated effort and prayer on your part to make a great humanitarian out of you by being a "good" wife and mother.

I think there are some things we can do to help our husbands in the way of admiration—things like commending him for his manliness, his masculinity. You can admire him for his strength and for his body structure. If he doesn't have a good physique, then you can find something else. How about his sexual abilities or leadership? Is he a good provider? You can admire his intellect and his achievements. You should be giving life to these with your words of positive confession. It will help him in the soul man. You can be sure if you are *not* telling him these things, someone else will be, especially if he is a man who is going places and doing things.

This reminds me of a woman who was in one of our classes. She told me she and her husband had been separated for six months. The Lord showed her exactly what had happened to split them up. He was a top executive for a very big corporation in our city. He traveled all over the world, spending a lot of time in the Orient and Europe; a lot of time away from home. This was his job. There were times he would ask her to go with him, but she wouldn't go. She refused to entrust "her" children to anyone else, even for a couple of weeks. Every time he went to his office to work, there was that little secretary, telling him what a "super salesman" he was—"Boy, do you look sharp today! I sure do like your suit!" Or, "Oh, I like your new hairstyle," or, "You sure swung that deal, what a mastermind you are!"

All of these things were building him up day after day. To contrast this, when he would come home, his wife would say things like, "You forgot to take out the garbage like I told you to!" and things like that, majoring on the trivial shortcomings. Do you really believe he felt like a man around her? She never built him up. She was always tearing him down and showing him all the things he *wasn't* doing. She was always ready to TELL him his faults as a father and husband. While, on the other hand, his secretary was always ready to mention his good qualities. Guess who won him? You're right—the secretary.

This is not the only cause of friction in marriage, but perhaps seeing this will help stimulate you to be honest enough with yourself and your husband that you can become aware of your problems and correct them.

Did you know that in the United States more divorces took place than marriages last year? That's a pretty hard statistic to take. And what is more discouraging is the fact that many of them call themselves Christians. Building divorce cases on trivia—unwillingness to die to self—unwillingness to make our marriages committed to the Word of God—is bringing discredit to and blaspheming that Word.

We are not learning how to be deceptive to win a man, nor are we wanting to keep him by doing all of these things. That thought may come to you at this point, and I have heard many women who have read different books on the woman's role and so forth say, "Oh, that is simply naive trash! It would never work!" I have to differ with them because I know it does work. I've tried it. Why shouldn't we use every idea, attitude, intellect or emotion to the advantage of our marriage?

As an English gentleman said once, "If it works, why fix it?" We're not learning how to be deceptive. We're learning to soul-minister by the power of the Holy Spirit, through our spirit. We are going to keep our husband! We're going to make these certain spiritual and soulish laws and principles become part of our natural character and personality. We want to have a corrected or an enhanced character. We want to be a good influence on everyone around us.

Remember, these simple principles not only apply to your husband, but also can be applied to your relationship with your son. He was made with exactly the same needs as your husband. He has a need for admiration and acceptance. He needs all the things that build up his masculinity and his male ego. He NEEDS those things. As a woman or a mother, you can be an influence to bring out the good in him.

Chapter Thirteen

Pride vs. the Male Ego

Is there a difference between pride and the male ego? Pride is defined as: "a boastful assurance of one's own resourcefulness."

The male ego may seem to be pride, but it's not. I believe that the male ego is what God has put into a man to catapult his natural drives and desires. His ego makes him want to take the initiative, to be the leader, the provider and the protector in the home. These are attitudes God has put into him. It isn't pride. Some men are prideful, but we need to make a separation. It took me a while to see that.

A wounded man is a man that has had his ego hurt. How many women have you heard say, "I can't get my husband to talk to me! He just won't talk to me," or "He just comes home from work and sits in front of the television and then he goes to bed." She was right when she said, "Talking to him is like talking to a wall." Her man may have built a wall around himself...it could be there for any one of a number of reasons. However, it can be broken down. There are things we can do to break it down.

1. Accept him just as he is.

2. Admire his masculinity (anywhere—from head to toe).

3. Stop degrading him.

4. Don't have a critical spirit of him or others.

5. When he confides in you, hold tight to those confidences and don't share them with anyone.

6. Notice him, regard him, honor him, prefer him, venerate and esteem him; defer to him, praise him and love and admire him exceedingly (see Eph. 5:33).

We had a lady in one of our classes that was really having a hard time with her husband. She was older than most of the students; around fifty-five or sixty. She came really desiring to have a better marriage. She knew she wasn't happy. She had no companionship with her husband at all. She shared with us one night: "He just brings boxes full of machinery home and leaves them in the living room, and he works on machines in the middle of the floor!" We all just roared with laughter, each of us thankful we didn't have to put up with the smell of grease in our living rooms. It wasn't funny to her. His entire life and interests were built around machinery. He never paid any attention to his dear little wife. We suggested she go home and tell him how much she appreciated all the money he was saving by fixing the machines himself. We told her to tell him how *smart* he was to be able to put them back together. Then, she, on her own initiative, bought some bows and stuck them on his boxes—all those boxes of greasy machinery in HER living room. It smelled like grease and dirt, but, in the wisdom of God, she soul-ministered to him by putting the bows on the boxes and told him how proud she was of him.

You know, about a week or two after that, she came to class and said, "You'll never guess what happened. This may not mean much to you, but my husband bought me a little picture to hang on my wall. He hasn't bought me one gift during our entire marriage! Oh, it's the prettiest little picture!"

She was so excited. He loved the attention she paid, showing how she appreciated him. It really meant a lot, and he responded to her. All she wanted was his love! It was really neat! Such a normal, "earthy" thing. I hope this will help you, too, to understand your husband. Men are different than women, and understanding them is something we have to learn.

They think differently. They have pressing responsibilities. We have to understand this. A man gives up freedom when he takes on a wife and family. He knows he must provide for them *for the rest of his life*. It is a big responsibility for a man and a hard thing for him to face sometimes. It places pressure on him, especially if he is having any difficulties doing it. If he isn't really making much money, or if he isn't progressing into the business world like he thinks he should, it produces pressure. We have to understand. Even if the wife is working outside the home to help out, he still feels the pressure of the responsibility being his. In comparison, few women give enough. When you relate what you are giving up to what he is giving up, you're not really laying aside much at all. When you marry a man, you expect him to be the leader, the provider and the protector. You're underneath his covering, so to speak, of leadership, provision and protection. You are not giving up anything; you are gaining everything. All the responsibility is going to be on his shoulders. Also, we need to understand what his attitude is and that he has a desire for status and must take his place in the world of men. You have to understand this to be able to help him.

He has to fulfill the purpose that God has called him to, whether it's doctor, lawyer, merchant, mechanic, evangelist, teacher or whatever. He must fulfill God's purpose for his life. Remember this: HE WANTS TO

BE A HERO IN YOUR EYES. HE REALLY DOESN'T CARE WHAT THE SECRETARY SAYS, but if you let it go long enough at home, he'll start listening. He wants to be a hero in your eyes. He wants to be your "knight in shining armor," just as much as you want to be a "Cinderella." Remember that and encourage him, love him and honor him.

Welcome him home! Let him know you understand he has had a hard day at work. Don't rush to the door and immediately tell him all the terrible things that have happened to you all day long, even though I know this is our first impulse. "Oh, if you just could have been here. You can't possibly understand what happened to me today!" There you stand, complete with pots boiling over. So, your day didn't go right. Your first concern should be for *him*. How did HIS day go?

Let him know you're glad that he's home. Let him tell you about HIS hard day.

A friend of mine who teaches a class on the woman's role said she really tried hard to be organized during the day. That way, she wouldn't be "on the go" quite so much right at supper time. She had time to fix herself up a bit before he came home from work. She had dinner prepared enough so when he came home, they could both go into the living room, sit down and have a cup of tea together—alone. It didn't take much more than fifteen minutes, but she said it was really surprising what it did for him. He would begin unloading his day. It really helped his ego because he could see she appreciated what he had been doing all day FOR HER (because he IS out there making money for her, you know)!

If you make him the king, he's going to make you the queen of your house. Of course, Jesus is number one and is the spiritual Head of each person in your household, but your husband is the head of your *home*. We are going to make him number one. We honor him in his position, not because we have to, but we know that when we "do" the Word of God, then all the natural laws of the soul and body fall into place and cause us to prosper.

There are some things that women tend to put first, before honoring their husbands. They honor their children much more than they should. It seems that in many cases the children receive favor in situations rather than the husband. You know, if he says, "Let's go somewhere," and she says, "Oh, but the children!" She puts them first, instead of saying, "All right, I'll get someone to take care of the children, and then I can go with you." He wouldn't have asked her in the first place if he didn't want her to go!

There are times when you won't be able to arrange for the children to be taken care of (and of course, we don't want them to be neglected), but sometimes you can. I know some women who don't even try because they have almost made idols out of their children, leaving dear Hubby out. It's really important that you don't listen to the devil when he whispers in your ear, "You are neglecting your children because you're going off with your husband."

This is wrong thinking. You need time alone with your husband and he needs time alone with you. I remember one woman whose husband traveled all over the world. He asked her to go with him many times, but she wouldn't. They had four children. She felt the responsibility of her children was more important than her responsibility to him. Their marriage was at stake and she should have gone (they had enough money for a sitter), but she didn't. Of course, she realized all of this much too late and lost her husband.

Also, as a wife, we have to consider the fact that someday our children are going to grow up and leave home. Think about it. That will leave just the two of you at home. In many marriages the husband has "hung in there" for as long as he can take it. The twenty years the children were at home are gone. When they leave, he says, "All right, good-bye, I've had it! I've helped you raise the kids..." and away he goes. They didn't spend enough time building their husband-wife relationship. That happens 80 percent of the time in American marriages right now. It's because the wife pays too much attention to the children's activities and desires, making them number one, instead of the husband. Sometimes, wives put homemaking, clubs, their appearance or even their career first—or it could be their parents. I'm not saying you are not to honor your father and mother. I think it is important even after you're married to honor your father and mother, but the Scriptures also tell us (see Gen. 2:24; Mark 10:6 –9) that we leave our parents, become one flesh and cleave to our husbands (or wives). We can be as obedient as possible to our parents. We can listen to their suggestions and love them, but when it comes right down to it, your husband's decisions should be the ones you go by. You should obey him even if he is making a mistake (unless he is going into sin—that's a different area altogether).

If he wants you to sin, you have to take your stand. Stay on the Lord's side because He's on your side, and He'll work it out for you.

All of the things we've mentioned are important, but you must give them the proper priority. Your husband has to take the place of honor. There are three good Scripture verses concerning this:

"Let your love be sincere—a real thing; hate what is evil (loathe all ungodliness, turn in horror from wickedness), but hold fast to that which is good. Love one another with brotherly affection—as members of one family—giving precedence and showing honor to one another" (Rom. 12:9–10).

We know that this is speaking to all believers but how much *more* should it apply to our husbands. We want to give preference to him in showing honor. "Out-do" what he's doing toward us, in showing honor back to him.

"However, let each man of you (without exception) love his wife as [being in a sense] his very own self; and let the wife see that she respects and reverences her husband—that she notices him, regards him, honors him, prefers him, venerates and esteems him, and that she defers to him, praises him, and loves and admires him exceedingly" (Eph. 5:33).

As I have said before and I will say again, I know that it takes the power of the Holy Spirit working through us for us to be obedient to this spiritual law. But, of course, when we are obedient to it, we then reap happiness in the soul and body realm. If he is not loving you as much as "his very own self " look to see if your attitudes and emotions have been good and that you haven't become a thorn in his side, not allowing him the freedom to love you.

"But I want you to know and realize that Christ is the head of every man, the head of a woman (wife) is her husband, and the Head of Christ is God" (1 Cor. 11:3, parentheses mine).

Here is another spiritual law which says to us that we are to honor the head of our home.

Some wives have committed idolatry! I didn't think I had, until I read Shirley Boone's book *One Woman's Liberation*. She shared how the Lord had shown her that her husband, Pat, had become an idol in her life. She absolutely idolized him. She loved him so much that her entire life was enveloped by him. No matter what he did, she was affected by it. Her worship of him was committing idolatry because she was putting him before her relationship with the Lord.

Shirley and I both discovered you must depend solely on your relationship with the Lord to receive *real* happiness, peace and joy. No matter how much you love your husband or any human, they are *imperfect* and will not always measure up to your ideas. When you put them in a more important place in your life than the Lord, you open yourself for many disappointments which can damage your marriage relationship.

Beware that this does not happen in your marriage. Don't make your husband an object of worship. Give him the love, honor, acceptance and admiration that is his due, but DON'T WORSHIP HIM. We aren't to carry things that far, but we are to minister to his needs in spirit, soul and body.

The results of idolatry are possessiveness—not giving him the freedom to do what he wants to do. Remember that God gave him his freedom of choice to determine right from wrong. If God gives man and woman the right to choose, then we as wives should also be able to give our man the right to choose—EVEN IF HE IS MAKING A MISTAKE! God does not stop us when we choose to make mistakes. We have the freedom to choose right or wrong. According to the spiritual guidelines set before us, when we do choose to do wrong, we can come back to God through repentance.

Never make the mistake of saying, "I told you so," after your man does something you had advised him not to do. If you say this or even have that attitude, it will close the doors of communication and make him feel intimidated. At that point he already *knows* he has made a mistake—even if he doesn't admit it to you. If you have a good relationship with him, there will be the day he will confess it to you as a mistake and he will find your understanding and forgiveness, bringing total reconciliation. This is a natural-soulish law which is initiated because of a spiritual law working in your spirit and soul.

We REACT differently when we are idolizing (and wanting to possess) something or someone. We have some of the following reactions:
1. Feelings of being neglected
2. Demanding our own way
3. Making threats
4. Clamming up

5. Giving him the cool treatment

6. Giving him all the facts, trying to make him feel obligated to be or do whatever it is you want him to be or do

Having these feelings or reactions means you have made him too important in your life — the extreme. It means you may fall into sin, following him rather than the Lord. Loving a man more than we love our Lord is a very dangerous position. Mark 12:30 –31 says:

"And you shall love the Lord your God out of and with your whole heart, and out of and with all your soul (your life) and out of and with all your mind—[that is] with your faculty of thought and your moral understanding—and out of and with all your strength. This is the first and principal commandment."

We desire to make Jesus number one!

Chapter Fourteen

Feminine Childlike Trust

We need to learn feminine dependency. This is an attitude of "child-like-ness," not "child-ish-ness." There is a difference between having a childlike attitude of trusting, and acting like a child, unable to accept your responsibilities. Being dependent is an area where you can express faith in your man. He delights in protecting and sheltering a woman who *needs* his manly care. It makes him FEEL GOOD to protect you, to shelter you. You should let "chivalry live" and *let* him protect! Let him do the heavy jobs and accept the heavy responsibilities.

It's easy to walk out from under this principle of need and response. Sometimes we would rather go ahead and do it ourselves (lacking patience), rather than try to figure a way to help him see the need and how he could do it. We may be more apt to encourage him in this direction if we could realize that the results of *letting* him be a "man" ministers so much life to his soul, which in turn will cause him to minister to your "woman" soulish needs.

I emphasize the term "let" because we, in most cases, have the power to allow him the opportunity or not.

LET him open doors for you. LET him have the financial responsibilities. LET him make the final decisions. Don't you be running things. Let him know he's the big, strong man in your life and how smart he is to make such good decisions. Let him know by saying it with your mouth! With that childlike attitude of trusting him, let him make his few mistakes...DON'T BE PUSHY, AND DON'T INSIST ON YOUR OWN WAY.

In 1 Corinthians 13:4 –7, Paul speaks about love:

"Love endures long and is patient and kind; love never is envious nor boils over with jealousy; is not boastful or vainglorious, does not display itself haughtily.

"It is not conceited—arrogant and inflated with pride; it is not rude (unmannerly), and does not act unbecomingly. Love [God's love in us] does not insist on its own rights or its own way, for it is not self-seeking; it is not touchy or fretful or resentful; it takes no account of the evil done to it—pays no attention to a suffered wrong.

"It does not rejoice at injustice and unrighteousness, but rejoices when right and truth prevail.

"Love bears up under anything and everything that comes, is ever ready to believe the best of every person, its hopes are fadeless under all circumstances and it endures everything [without weakening]."

This fruit of love, in its full meaning as stated, can help you to show that childlike trust in him. You cannot really bear up under all things, or believe what he says and does unless you have this childlike attitude of trust. This fruit is developed by the power of the Holy Spirit working through His Word which is hidden in your heart. The attitude of childlike trust is likened to our attitude toward God. We look to Him as our Father. We trust Him. We believe in Him, and we have patience for the answers that come from Him. This same type of love relationship or attitude is what you can have toward your husband. Your being dependent upon him gives him a "good feeling." You are ministering to him in a soul-ministry. It makes him feel good because he knows you know he DOES have the power to protect you. It makes him feel stronger, more competent, more confident, more manly. It will help him to fulfill his role as a successful husband. You have helped bring him right up to this satisfying feeling by having that childlike attitude, supporting his judgment in all things and letting him have the responsibility for the results of his decisions. All of these things are avenues for a closer relationship.

We want our spirit to control the soul. Remember if we don't have victory in our attitudes and our emotions, then look for the works of the flesh, come to repentance, receive forgiveness from God and yourself and get back into right relationship and the Word of God. Renew your mind, and the victory will come. The fruit of the Spirit must *flow* from you to minister life to your husband. When you start having arguments (heated discussions), resentments and lack of victory, the works of the flesh are operating in your marriage. You have to *willfully* determine to turn to God in prayer (your husband, too, if he is a believer). Repent to each other, and repent to God. Let the Word of God renew your mind. The Holy Spirit will bring revelation knowledge to your mind through the Word. It is a cleansing agent. It will bring forth the fruit of the Holy Spirit resulting in the ministering of life and not death with the POWER OF THE TONGUE.

It is very important to have open communication lines. Communication has two elements: 1) talking, and 2) listening. Talking and listening must be exercised by the wife as well as the husband for total success. If your husband has trouble communicating, perhaps it is because you have allowed *reactions* (bad attitudes and emotions) to cover up the real problems and are not really able to express your need. He may not feel you trust him enough and therefore he has fear in opening up to you, perhaps a fear of being ridiculed or shown his faults. Once real trust is established we *can* communicate and express our faults one to another. This trust is oftentimes killed by marriage partners who, in a moment of complete disappointment, discouragement, frustration and feelings of hopelessness will blurt out these words, "It's not going to work, we might as well get a divorce." Once this word "divorce" has been given life (the power of the tongue), you can be *sure* the devil will use it for the destruction of your marriage.

It is absolutely essential that if "divorce" has been spoken of by you or your mate in a heated argument or otherwise, that you take time to reassure each other that deep in your heart you know that divorce is neither the answer nor the desire of your heart and you are determined to work things out. Reaffirm your love toward each other. This must be done *even if you cannot agree on the outward circumstances*. Trust *must* be renewed.

Every word you speak can bring life! Let them bring forth life and not death. Proverbs 31:26 says:

"She opens her mouth with skillful and godly wisdom, and in her tongue is the law of kindness—giving counsel and instruction."

Her tongue is speaking wisdom and knowledge, in kindness.

Never stop loving and giving, for loving and giving come out of the soul. If you don't let it come out of your soul, you will become bitter and cynical. Don't ever stop loving, no matter how tough it gets. You may not *like* what he is doing, but *love* him anyway. Don't stop giving yourself. Otherwise, you will let bitterness and resentment come in. As a wife, mother and woman, you need to plant seeds of love, praise, truth, confidence, admiration and so forth in your home. These seeds will produce life—exactly what we will harvest in return: LIFE.

You will receive praise from your husband. He will say, "You are the most excellent. You excel them all." Just like the virtuous woman in Proverbs 31. This is what we want, isn't it? This is our reward. We will reap what we sow.

Philippians 4:8–9 says to THINK on these things: those things that are lovely, good, honorable, just, pure, kind and of a good report. Those are the things that should constantly be spoken of in our homes. The Amplified Bible says, "**fix your mind on them.**"

Finally, in thinking of childlike trust, I want to comment on unsaved husbands. Romans 2:4 says:

"**...Are you unmindful or actually ignorant [of the fact] that God's kindness is intended to lead you to repent—to change your mind and inner man to accept God's will?**"

Here God is manifesting Himself in "kindness" (a fruit of the Spirit).

God operates in kindness to lead us to repentance. The fruit of kindness is not preaching the Word at your unsaved husband, nor is it telling him all his faults, but it is the ACT OF SHOWING him you care. It will bring him to repentance.

That is why 1 Peter 3:1–2 says:

"**In like manner you married women, be submissive to your own husbands—subordinate yourselves as being secondary to and dependent on them, and adapt yourselves to them. So that even if any do not obey the Word [of God], they may be won over not by discussion but by the [godly] lives of their wives, when they observe the pure and modest way in which you conduct yourselves, together with your reverence [for your husband. That is, you are to feel for him all that reverence includes]—to respect, defer to, revere him; [revere means] to honor, esteem** (appreciate, prize), and [in the human sense] adore him; [and adore means] to admire, praise, be devoted to, deeply love and enjoy [your husband]."

The wife's behavior, love and fellowship is body-soul ministry to him. If the wife does all the things we have discussed in the soul areas, as well as what we will discuss in the body area, the Holy Spirit is free to work through her with the fruits her man can see. It will bring him to repentance, and right on into the kingdom of God. He doesn't have a chance! Glory to God!

One of the best examples I have heard of in this area was Smith Wigglesworth's wife. He was by trade a plumber who was in a backslidden condition for a number of years who later became a famous minister of the Gospel. He went "all out" for God, evangelizing, casting out demons, laying hands on the sick and seeing them recover. His wife had lived with him for many years, simply being a GOOD and godly wife. She gave him a happy home.

The part of the story I would like to emphasize here begins on a day when she had taken good care of him, had given him his dinner and put everything in order. She had paid a lot of attention to him, and, having done all this, she told him that she wanted to leave to go to church. He said, "No. You spend too much time at church. If you go to church, I will lock the doors and you won't be able to get back inside." She told him, "Well, Smith, I have to go to church! I love the Lord and He said for us not to forsake the assembling of ourselves together." She needed the fellowship of other believers. So she went on to church, having fulfilled her body-soul ministry to him. She loved him. Smith was being cantankerous, that was all. She went on to church, came home, and sure enough, he had locked every door. She didn't have a key so she couldn't get in. She took her coat, pulled it up over her, and sitting at the back door, stayed there all night.

In the morning she could hear him getting up. Not

too much later, he came out, opened the door, and looked at her. She jumped up and said, "Good morning, Smith! What would you like for breakfast?" Now that's an attitude!

That's what you call being humble. Look at the results. God took that humility and exalted her. Because of the kindness and love she showed to him, body-soul ministering to him, he came to the Lord and was filled with the Holy Spirit. He became one of the greatest faith-men known in our time.

She gave us a good example, didn't she? Submissiveness is something that you give. It cannot be demanded. It is an attitude of the heart. YOU have to decide to be submissive.

We have given you natural principles and spiritual laws as to why you should submit, but submission is your decision. NO MAN WILL ULTIMATELY RESPECT YOU IF HE IS ALLOWED TO WALK ON YOU. Here, balance comes up again.

Remember, there is a difference between being submissive and being a doormat. In counseling we have heard many women say things like, "My husband didn't want me to come to the meeting (or to church) because he wanted me to do so and so with him." Well, some of this won't hurt anything, but if you make a habit of putting your fellowship with man before your fellowship with God, you will quickly find yourself in a backslidden condition.

A Christian wife must hold true to her commitment to the Lord. If it has to be at the cost of losing her unbelieving husband because he can no longer subject himself to her love for God, then the Word says she is free.

"But if the unbelieving partner [actually] leaves, let him do so; in such [cases the remaining] brother or sister is not morally bound. But God has called us to peace" (1 Cor. 7:15).

Please notice the believing wife is to body-soul

minister to her husband (read all of 1 Corinthians 7), doing *all* she can to keep her marriage intact.

Remember, if you are in the right—God sides with you!

PART THREE

Our Ministry in the Body

Chapter Fifteen

Abundant Wholeness

Jesus said that He came to give us an *abundant life.*

"The thief comes only in order that he may steal and may kill and may destroy. I came that they may have and enjoy life, and have it in abundance—to the full, till it overflows" (John 10:10).

We have an abundant life to expect! There are many Christians who don't know they should expect an abundant life. I didn't until I became a *believer*, and my ears became opened to the truth of the Word. It is easier to understand the abundant life principles if we understand God and His ways, ourselves—who we are and of what we are made.

To reiterate, we know that God is three Persons—Father, Son and Holy Spirit—the holy Godhead. God is triune, just as we as human beings are triune (created in His image and likeness). We are spirit, soul and body. Once we become born again, our spirit comes alive to

God and becomes new (see 1 Cor. 5:17). It is then that the soul must become subject to the spirit, which lives in "the temple of the Holy Spirit," the body.

To be *one* person, just as God is *one* Person, we must bring the body into subjection to our spirit, just as we shared in previous chapters that our soul must be subject to our spirit.

The body, then, is the five senses—hearing, seeing, smelling, tasting and feeling. Since our body does what our mind, intellect and will says to do, it is imperative that we get our mind on the side of God. The battleground area of the enemy is the soul, or the mind. This is what we really need to understand. The will, our decision-maker, is positioned here. We are constantly being fed, either with intellectual knowledge, the lies of Satan, or with the Word of God. Our will decides what we are going to believe. If we believe the lies of Satan, not rejecting them, these thoughts will go into our soul (mind and intellect) and be read by our spirit. They will be computed in our spirit and will come out of us through our soul and body in the form of unbelief, doubt and other *negative responses*.

On the other hand, if we believe the Word of God and feed it into our soul, our intellect and mind; if we let *it* become part of our attitudes and emotions; if, by our will, we digest the Word of God, and *it* goes down into our spirit and is computed, it will come out of us in faith, power and other *positive responses* (see Matt. 12:34,37). When we understand this, we can more readily have victory in our lives as Christians and have exactly what Jesus said—*that abundant life.* Wholeness! We want to learn in every way we can, not from one person only, or one Scripture verse, but continuously learning from the entire Word of God and the multitude of ministries (apostles, prophets, evangelists, teachers, pastors) He has placed in the body of Christ to minister to us.

Proverbs 18:21 says:

"Death and life are in the power of the tongue and they who indulge it shall eat the fruit of it [for death or life]."

When we speak negative things, we produce negative responses. For instance, suppose I told you I thought you looked sick today, or that you looked tired; if you are willing to submit to those words, they can make you start thinking you are sick. Negative words in extreme cases can cause sickness and in more subtle cases can cause you to feel pretty low. Unless YOUR WILL rejects those negative words and says, "No! In Christ, I'm healed," "I have His strength," "The Word of God says I am not going to fail," "I can do ALL things through Christ," "I am a beautiful person, the Word says I am," or "I am the righteousness of God in Christ," and in this way block out the lies, you may be overcome by the negative words of death.

So we must remember then, that all the words we speak have the potential to produce life or death. We want "life words" to operate from our body. The principles we will talk about are principles you can use to win a man if you are single, or if you are already married, you can use them to keep him. As a Christian woman, I want to keep the man I have, not only because I love him and need him but because the Word says I *must* keep him until we leave our earthly body.

Each area of us—spirit, soul or body—influences each of the other two areas. What we want to do is get the right part of us in control! The right part is the spirit man. We want him—the hidden man of the heart—to be in control.

Chapter Sixteen

The Virtuous Woman

In speaking of the virtuous woman, a good wife, Solomon in Proverbs 31:10 writes:

"A capable, intelligent and virtuous woman, who is he who can find her? She is far more precious than jewels, and her value is far above rubies or pearls."

This statement is confirmed in 1 Corinthians 11:7, where it says, **"...but woman is [the expression of] man's glory (majesty, pre-eminence)."** She is the glory of her man because she is the extension of his purpose. She is a reflection of his successes (and if she is a good wife she hides or covers his failures with her love). This constitutes her being the glory of HER man.

In the eleventh verse of Proverbs 31 it goes on:

"The heart of her husband trusts confidently in her and relies on and believes in her safely, so that he has no lack of honest gain or need of dishonest spoil."

He trusts her because they are united in spirit, soul and body. They have come into agreement for their purpose in life which brings forth trust. He knows she will not undermine their dreams. She will carefully and prudently take care of their material goods and finances so they can build their future. He knows that in her heart she is "content" and they both can say with Paul (Phil. 4:11)... **"I have learned how to be content (satisfied to the point where I am not disturbed or disquieted) in whatever state I am. I know how to be abased and live humbly in strained curcumstances, and I know also how to enjoy plenty and live in abundance.**

"She will comfort, encourage and do him only good as long as there is life within her" (v. 12). She builds him up, verbalizing her faith in him. She becomes a Holy Spirit filled vessel of supportive power to him.

"She seeks out the wool and flax and works with willing hands to develop it" (v. 13).

Her attitude is that of submission, allowing him to make decisions and take the responsibilities. I don't mean that she doesn't make some decisions. In other words, her life is not just a cop-out. There are some women who have been made to believe that *any* place of submission to their husband is a place where they have no voice and no responsibilities. This is far from being true, and if we watch to see exactly what this virtuous woman is doing, we're going to see that she has a lot of decisions to make, and she takes responsibility.

"She is like the merchant ships loaded with food stuffs, she brings her household's food from a far [country]. She rises while yet it is night and gets spiritual food for her household and assigns her maids their tasks" (vv. 14–15).

There is much to be done. She has maids to help but has to know how to plan their duties in order for them to be of help to her. She's an organized woman. Also, she has made time for her personal devotions with the Lord and sought after "spiritual food" for her household. To me this is the intercession she makes each day in her spiritual language for her family, overthrowing and destroying strongholds of the enemy (see 2 Cor. 10:4).

"She considers a new field before she buys or accepts it—expanding prudently [and not courting neglect of her present duties by assuming others]. With her savings [of time and strength] she plants fruitful vines in her vineyard" (v. 16).

She's no dummy! She is a business woman for the sake of her household. She is a worker!

"She girds herself with strength [spiritual, mental and physical fitness for her God-given tasks] and makes her arms strong and firm" (v. 17).

She accepts the fact that she is a triune person and has responsibilities to herself in the spirit, soul and body.

As we read these next verses, meditate on them and see what the Holy Spirit is saying to you.

"She tastes and sees that her gain from work [with and for God] is good; her lamp goes not out, but it burns on continually through the night [of trouble, privation or sorrow, warning away fear, doubt, and distrust]. She lays her hands to the spindle, and her hands hold the distaff.

"She opens her hand to the poor: yea, she reaches out her filled hands to the needy [whether in body, mind or spirit].

"She fears not the snow for her family, for all her household are doubly clothed in scarlet.

"She makes for herself coverlets cushions and rugs of tapestry. Her clothing is of linen, pure and white and fine, and of purple [such as that of which the clothing of the priests and the hallowed cloth of the temple are made].

"Her husband is known in the city's gates, when he sits among the elders of the land.

"She makes fine linen garments and leads others to buy them; she delivers to the merchants girdles [or sashes that free one for service].

"Strength and dignity are her clothing and her position is strong and secure. She rejoices over the future—the later day or time to come [knowing that she and her family are in readiness for it].

"She opens her mouth with skillful and godly wisdom, and in her tongue is the law of kindness—giving counsel and instruction.

"She looks well to how things go in her household, and the bread of idleness [gossip, discontent and self-pity] she will not eat" (vv. 18–27).

We see that this virtuous woman has the positive attributes of strength and dignity, knowing the role she is to fulfill in her home and feeling strong and secure in this position. Her mind transmits wisdom and kindness so that through her mouth come words of good counsel and instruction, refusing to fellowship with thoughts and words of gossip, discontent and self-pity which could destroy her and her household.

Now we can look at the effect all of these virtues have had on those around her—look at this positive response!

"Her children rise up and call her blessed [happy, fortunate, and to be envied]; and her husband boasts of and praises her, saying, 'many daughters have done virtuously, nobly and well [with the strength of character that is steadfast in goodness] but you excel them all.'

"Charm and grace are deceptive, and beauty is vain [because it is not lasting], but a woman who reverently and worshipfully fears the Lord, she shall be praised!

"Give her of the fruit of her hands, and let her own work praise her in the gates of the city!"

Isn't that beautiful? Oh, hallelujah! It is such a wonderful reward to hear our children and our man *say* that. To *know* that he thinks you "excel them all" is such a compliment, and when he comes to you and says, "you're really great," "you're the GREATEST!" "I'm so glad you're mine"—don't you know our woman heart leaps for joy to know we have fulfilled our role in his eyes, and that he believes you are truly a gift from God.

Chapter Seventeen

Inner Beauty

To successfully have the outward appearance of radiance, vibrance and happiness, we must also have inner peace. As Christians we have learned by the Word and by experience that peace is acquired by development in the soul and spirit areas. When our character, which is made up of our attitudes, emotions, will and intellect begins falling in line with the Word of God, our spirit comes to be at peace and rest with God, ourselves and others. When there is peace on the inside, there will be an outward manifestation of it, and we will be at rest in all areas of our life. The object then, is to have the spirit controlling the body and soul. I can't emphasize that enough. Before we are born again, the soul and the body are in control. The spirit is quenched and hindered inside of us. Unless you were born again when you were very, very small, and had proper teaching, knowing positive responses and who you are in Christ Jesus, your spirit probably hasn't fully developed.

So if you are unhappy and you do not have inner peace, chances are that:

1. You cannot accept yourself.

2. You are having trouble accepting others.

3. Your happiness is dependent on other people and the way they treat you (for example, the way your husband treats you, the way your children or your friends treat you).

4. You depend on surrounding circumstances for happiness, such as more money, social status, physical beauty, new clothes, sharp car, beautiful house and so forth.

5. You think that if you had less pressure and less responsibility you could be happier.

All of these things mean that you are looking to the flesh and to the five senses for comfort and happiness.

Happiness and inner peace come only through Christ Jesus. In order to have a character change, we must have a right relationship with God. Having that relationship we can learn to accept ourselves and others, just as we are, faults and all. That is a big accomplishment. This does not mean that we will not seek improvement or expect others to improve.

In finding inner peace, we find joy, which is a fruit of the Spirit. Joy brings strength to our character. It also brings right attitudes and emotions. In Nehemiah 8:10 it says:

"...and be not grieved and depressed for the joy of the Lord is our strength, and stronghold."

And my, how many times does a wife and mother need additional strength? You'll find that inner strength comes by the Spirit, and the fruit of the Spirit. Strength is the fruit of joy. The joy of the Lord is our strength! So, knowing joy, spiritual joy, because He is the Lord of our lives, and knowing all of our needs are met in Him brings us happiness and inner peace.

This means knowing our spiritual place in Christ Jesus, and our position in high places with Him:

"But God, who is rich in mercy, for his great love wherewith he loved us, even when we were dead in sins, hath quickened us together with Christ, (by grace ye are saved;) and hath raised us up together, and made us sit together in heavenly places in Christ Jesus: that in the ages to come he might shew the exceeding riches of his grace in his kindness toward us through Christ Jesus" (Eph. 2:4–7, KJV).

When you finally realize down in your spirit that you are sitting with Jesus by the throne of God, what greater joy could you possibly have? All the power, all the strength, all the health, all the provisions for life are yours because *you are in Christ Jesus*. This gives you inner happiness. You have to know this. You have to know it down in your spirit, and the only way you are going to get it into your spirit is by the Word of God being "computerized" into you, and coming out as faith, power and positive responses in your life.

Joy does not know anything about happiness. Happiness is a fleshly thing. Joy comes from the spirit. Joy is a spiritual force. It could care less what the physical senses say or what the circumstances are. When you feel down and out, or even if at night when you husband says, "Honey, mmm!" and you feel like "Let's go to sleep!" the joy of the Lord can manifest in your spirit to come through that body and give you the strength you need to minister to your husband in body ministry. That's just a plain old practical situation, and it happens in most houses every night. So let's apply it where we can use it. An automatic response to inner peace, then, is a smile and a pleasant countenance. Remember again, that this glowing, fresh contented appearance is appealing to your husband.

Do you want him to pay attention to you? Then be appealing to him. You have to make your body appealing to your husband. You may have wondered why there are so many temptations to our men. Outside of our homes, other women are making themselves appealing. This should challenge you. You have to maintain appeal even in your own house. It doesn't mean that every day you have to go around like a raving beauty, but there does have to be some semblance of beauty—a happy, fresh, vibrant appearance that is appealing to him, letting the "Sonshine" out. Think about it. There will not be one person that is going to want to look at that woman if she looks sad, depressed, dejected and disheveled, and say, "I like to be with you," or "I want what you have!" As we allow the Holy Spirit to work through our spirit to manifest this joy and peace in our body, on our face, in our eyes and in everything about us, we will glorify God in our bodies.

"Let not yours be the [merely] external adorning with [elaborate] interweaving and knotting of the hair, the wearing of jewelry, or changes of clothes; but let it be the inward adorning and beauty of the hidden person of the heart, with the incorruptible and unfading charm of a gentle and peaceful spirit, which (is not anxious or wrought up, but) is very precious in the sight of God. For it was thus that the pious women of old who hoped in God were (accustomed) to beautify themselves, and were submissive to their husbands—adapting thenselves to them as secondary and dependent upon them" (1 Peter 3:3–5).

Chapter Eighteen

Homemakers Indeed

The second chapter of Titus says, **"...wisely train the young women to be...homemakers."**

It is for sure we can use all the help we can get when there are so many demands on our time as wife, mother, friend and so forth.

Being organized is the greatest asset. Some women start backing off when you suggest "being ORGANIZED", as it suggests work and ways of doing things that are different than the way "mother" taught or are different than the way they are doing it now and they resist change. But this is one secret in keeping your husband happy.

For those who are "beginners" in organizing their day, I would suggest that you prepare a list. This can be done the night before if you have time, or even as you work during the day. Write down duties for the next day as they come to you. Pray over your list. Did you ever think of that? Ask the Lord to show you what you really need to do tomorrow. The list needs to be made, keeping in mind that the duties should be in order of their real importance.

First, it is important for you to make time for YOU, your appearance and exercise. This is the first body duty (not your first priority—that should be your devotion with the Lord at the beginning of the day). This will make you start your day off feeling and looking great. Your spirit is in tune and your physical appearance is pleasing. Then plan another short time of "freshening up" just before your man comes home.

Number two has two parts:

Part 1: Give priority to the jobs delegated by your husband. The big ones are not hard to remember, but sometimes it is easy to miss the little jobs. He may just say, "The button came off my shirt. Here is the shirt and the button. Would you sew it on for me?" It is easy for us to classify this as a minor job and mentally put it at the bottom of the list. With major things coming up all day (maybe two or three), it is easy to forget the button and his shirt. Later, when he wants to wear it, the button isn't on it! And a very simple thing that wouldn't have taken but a minute is not done. To him it had some priority and therefore you could have "made points" with him by giving first place to something that was important to him that day. When we don't do these little things which are important to him, it makes him think, "Why can't she do a simple thing like sewing on a button for me?" Believe it or not, he can have resentment against the other things you do, whether they are worthy causes or not, when he feels neglected. Our excuse could have been legitimate to us, like cleaning the big dirty closet in the hall that you finally got to after months of trying. You know the one; the next time someone opens it, you anticipate everything falling out.

Part 2: Give priority to the most unpleasant jobs you have for the day. These should be done while you have the most energy.

Number three, try to have just one major project each day, so that you have time for your daily routine tasks. This works pretty well.

Number four, if possible, begin to plan and prepare dinner right after breakfast, especially if you are a very active woman. You might have a meeting to attend, shopping to do, or children to taxi around. Unless we really get on top of our meal planning, the day can become all "jammed up" around dinnertime, and then we are throwing things together for dinner. This hint really helped me, and I found it to be a joy. I began to set the table for dinnertime after everyone had left for the day. (No one came home for lunch.) I put on the tablecloth, placemats and so forth. I even had a centerpiece. It looked nice, at least nicer than they previously were used to! I learned I could make the dessert, salad and some meat dishes early in the morning, and best of all I found that I was really organized by the time my husband came home, having to do only a few last-minute items. Also our meals became nutritionally more balanced.

I remember the first time my family came in and looked at the table after I had taken the opportunity to plan my meal early in the day. They said, "Ooh, who's coming to dinner?" taking a long look at the table with tablecloth, full place setting of silverware, dishes and a pretty centerpiece. I said, "No one, it's just for you!" That really made points. I can't tell you how many points that made! They really thought it was great— paying so much attention on their behalf. As we sat down to our table, I dimmed the lights and lit the candles. As our teenage boys sat there, I could feel that the candle-lit meal had a serene effect on them and even brought out the "gentlemen" in them.

Number five, add feminine touches around your house, such as flowers, or any one of the many things we can find that can "fuss up" a house a little bit, giving it a pleasant atmosphere and "good smell." Men relate

118

some smells with femininity—the smell of freshly baked cookies, cakes, pies, bread or even meat. (Really, anything that smells good). For my family it's fried onions. I remember one time, our son Jerry was clear down the street on his bicycle. I heard the front door slam and here he came, all out of breath! "Wow, Mom! I could smell whatever you're cooking all the way to the stop sign." It was a panful of onions. It really turned him on!

Number six is—WORK! Put that on your list. Put it in your mind also —WORK. And then DO IT! Stay with it until it's completed, whatever it is. Nothing can take the place of working. You have to get in there, sometimes with a lot of "elbow grease." There is always a great deal of satisfaction when we feel we have accomplished something.

Number seven, be careful of time wasted on shopping trips. This might be one of the things on your list: to go to the store. You can waste a lot of time at the store, walking up and down the aisles, looking. This is lots of fun when you have *lots* of time, but sometimes it can consume the best part of your day and leave you totally unorganized and exhausted. Also, there is a spirit that is ever present in every store. It's called the "buy, buy, buy, buy spirit." If you are having to watch your budget closely, you are going to have to watch out for that "spirit" because of the temptation to buy things which we do not need. It is good to make a grocery list and *follow it.* You'll come out money and time ahead. Another suggestion: don't grocery shop when you're hungry. It will tempt you to buy unnecessary items (usually junk food).

You know, successful businesses pay top money to have efficiency experts come into their offices and tell them how they can run at peak performance. Why shouldn't we as women, then, learn how to organize our homes so they can run efficiently also? We must have time with the Lord first, for ourselves, for our appearance, for our homemaking duties, for "R & R" (rest and relaxation), and then, happily, time left for our husbands and children.

The last thing, but one of the most important, is to have a "sensible attitude," in case events of our day change. This is really important. It also was a hard one for me because I was still overcoming a perfectionist attitude. I thought if I didn't get everything on my list done, it would ruin my entire day. But you can't have a rigid schedule or attitude when you have a family or those who may need your attention at a moment's notice. You have to remain flexible and adaptable, keeping a good attitude.

Every man appreciates a home that is in order, and a woman who is ready to meet him at the door when he comes home. Meet him happily with a big smile and bright eyes (even when he is late).

There is much joy in being a *successful* homemaker.

Chapter Nineteen

Should I Work Outside of My Home?

This can only be answered by you, depending on your circumstances and commitments. Also you must consider the need your husband has to be the successful provider in your home.

If you are a single woman, widow, divorcee or wife of a man who is disabled, you can feel confident in your justification to work outside of your home.

Ideally, it is not good for a married woman to work outside of her home when it takes away responsibility from her man or causes her not to fulfill her role of wife or mother. (Remember, you chose to make this "love covenant" with your man so you have a responsibility to keep it in line with the Word of God.)

DANGER!! Even though a husband may approve of his wife working outside of their home, there is still the likelihood that he will have to deal with feelings of inadequacy and dual role playing, which if not dealt with can cause serious marriage problems.

Other dangers come about when women have to

compete with men in the work world. This competitiveness causes them to treat her like a man, a fellow worker, and for this reason, many women have lost their femininity and charm and have brought home with them that aggressive, dominating spirit which causes them to become independent, capable and efficient!

Look at the Women's Liberation Movement: Femininity is on its way out...or is it? I believe we are in the majority, *WE* who want femininity and charm, because we know that it creates a desire in our man to protect and care for us and increases his feeling of masculinity.

The whole issue of the husband's feelings and reactions toward a working wife has been taken into focus by very few and completely omitted from the Women's Lib Movement or ERA (the Equal Rights Amendment).

Granted, there are some situations where it is *financially necessary* for the wife to take on a job outside her home, but there also are an equal amount of women who are doing it for *self-fulfillment* and some who are on a real "ego trip."

As working wives begin to thrust themselves forward in their independence on the job as well as at home, their husbands, whether they understand and support their wives or not, can suffer much anxiety in realizing that they have as much to lose as their wives have to gain in a career, with its satisfactions and pleasures. He may experience feelings of anger and confusion because of the changes occurring in their marriage.

He sees her moving away from the household chores and the ability she had, because of adequate time and a submissive attitude, to make their home a quiet, warm, good smelling, peaceful place and to do special things for the children and him. He also sees that, in all fairness, he must assume some of the workload at home (making him feel that he is taking on "woman's" work and he no longer is the head but an equal). And finally the husband is disturbed by the implications that he has failed in taking care of his family.

Unless the wife is very much aware of how he is feeling (his "male feelings") and handles it wisely, assuring him of his leadership role in their home and her desire to maintain a submissive role in this equal job opportunity world that we live in, she will experience marital problems.

Remember, the Scriptures say "the husband is to be the head of the wife" and when we break spiritual laws, as well as natural laws, we will most likely have serious problems.

Some wives who have turned in rebellion and rage from their traditional and scriptural role of "good wife" have done so because they listened to the deceptive lie that they have to be an "individual person" rather than the extension of their husband.

There are also women who refuse to humble themselves and find ways to help their husband succeed and take on his responsibilities which may have been neglected in the past. Most of them would rather wallow in self-pity and say to their husband, "I've been cleaning up after you and your kids for twenty years and I've hated every day of it—now it's your turn to see what it's like to be stuck in this house—I'm going out to make something of myself." They preferred to listen to the lie in Women's Lib that says, "Housewife, you're considered a second-rate citizen, and look at you, you have all those talents and skills."

True, as women we do have a great deal of intelligence, many talents and skills, but if we used them in our homes as we should, we would find self-satisfaction of a more pure kind. We would fulfill God's purpose for woman. There is real fulfillment plus the opportunity to teach and influence our children toward successful productive lives as well as supporting our husband in such a way that he cannot fail. Just because we are qualified to fill certain positions, does not mean we are *justified* in doing so!

Many women today feel trapped in their home or trapped in a bad marriage situation and make a decision to separate themselves from that situation by going to work. She decides that *freedom* is the *most* important thing in her life. However, later on we hear her say, "I am totally free, but I'm not sure that I haven't paid too high a price for it. Since, really, I have found I haven't had a free moment yet!"

The National Institute on Drug Abuse stated that an estimated:

a. Thirty-two million American women (42 percent) have used tranquilizers—compared to 19 million men (27 percent).

b. Sixteen million women (21 percent) have had sedatives prescribed for them—compared to 12 million men (17 percent).

c. Twelve million women have used stimulants—compared to 5 million men.

I believe that the woman's need for these drugs tells us the story of what's happening to her in today's world. The stresses of her demanding outside job and taking care of her family as well mount up to a 32-hour-a-day job, which is physically impossible to maintain (twenty-four hours for home and eight hours on the job outside).

Working outside our home divides our loyalty and our strength, preventing us from being that lovable, capable wife and mother. Many times the love and work that we do for our family is done in secret, many times unseen and unnoticed, but the reaping of that which was done in secret can be shown in the happiness, success and productivity of our family. The old saying, "Behind every successful man is a good wife" holds the same truth today as it did a hundred years ago or two thousand years ago.

My hat goes off to the woman who can *successfully*

maintain her role as wife, mother and homemaker, plus an eight-hour job. I know some have no choice, financially speaking, and as a word of encouragement for you who *must* do it, make this your confession: "I can do all things through Christ who strengthens me." Also, in remembering the natural laws concerning the attitudes, feelings and needs of your husband, you will be able to do what you have to do without risking your relationship.

I would like to leave this subject after asking you to ask yourself these two questions:

1. Are you working because it is a financial necessity or is it the continual drive to have a material status symbol?

2. Are you working for self-fulfillment when you would really like to find the same self-fulfillment at home, if you just felt your husband and family would appreciate what you're doing for them?

It is true that we all, male and female, have need of feeling fulfilled. When we do all things, no matter what our role is, unto the Lord, we will have success. We then can be the master over our situations and circumstances, instead of them being master over us.

Chapter Twenty

Study to Show Yourself Approved

Is it vital for a woman to have an education? Perhaps we would not have to use the word *vital* as it may seem too strong for some. However, an education is surely an asset to us even if we never use it professionally.

There is no doubt that if a woman remains single, is a divorcee or becomes a widow, an education could make the difference between success or failure in providing for herself and perhaps a number of children.

Regardless of our circumstances in life, it is of utmost importance to our own well–being that we continuously feel that we are needed and are creative persons.

Since we are made in the image and likeness of God, our Creator, He has made us to be "creators." If a male or female is not feeling fulfillment in this area of being creative, it can lead to serious problems of depression and emotional/physical disorders.

As a spiritual principle, God admonishes us to study

to make ourselves approved. He knows that if we lack the knowledge of His Word we cannot live in the prosperity of spirit, soul or body. We will, in fact, fall short of receiving every good thing He has provided for us if we don't *know how* we can obtain it. Third John 2 says:

"Beloved, I pray that you may prosper in every way and [that your body] may keep well, even as [I know] your soul keeps well and prospers."

The same is true in natural principles. If we do not have the natural knowledge which has been given to man, we could still be living in the stone age, so to speak, never prospering or being creative.

Unless you are having to be prepared in a skill or profession to work outside of your home, it may not be necessary for you to go back to school to receive more education. Much self-education can be done by keeping up with current world and community events, reading widely and being interested in people and activities outside of your own home.

An education will help us to manage our household more efficiently and give us a broader view of the society in which we live. Being educated can help us stimulate growth and interests of our children. Through educating ourselves we are able to relate to them, to their needs at home and away from home. We live in a society that is being educated, sometimes for good and sometimes for evil.

You can't really understand your child's problems and what he is having to cope with if you don't have an education or the experience to understand his circumstances. Everything you have learned combines to make you a more interesting companion, both for your children and your husband.

When your husband comes home all enthused about the events of his day and you sit there showing total ignorance or disinterest, your relationship is being hindered. Even if you don't understand, it's better to *learn* how to "draw him out" and make him feel good. Making him know you are interested in what he has been doing is important. Also, the more educationally well-rounded person you are, the more opportunity you will have had to be exposed to what he is going through or it may help you understand what his goals are in his own life, ultimately helping your purposes in life come together as "one." Remember, he has a great big world out there where he is in constant competition with other men, looking for success and self-worth, and he needs your understanding and encouragement.

Some women are really "duds" never knowing anything about anything. All they know is that they have to cook three meals a day and clean up! These women are in great danger of getting bored and depressed if they do not broaden their interests into every area of their house and every area of family and community living. I'm not knocking the "good cook," for this is one of the very best ways to please our husband and children. Besides, being creative with food is so much fun. Those of us who have had the privilege of being home full-time and have been creative with food know that preparing food from scratch is more healthy for us, more economical and more eye-appealing.

Knowing how to add and subtract, a part of our being educated, is certainly an asset to the homemaker who is conscious of keeping a balanced budget and making wise decisions at the market.

There are actually so many ways that we can be creative. Our activities can be very diversified. As a word of caution, however, never let the activities outside your home cause you to neglect the responsibilities in your home. Wait on the Lord as to your daily activities. Perhaps He may want you to spend time interceding for your family or others—or visit and pray for someone in the hospital. You need to train yourself to be sensitive to the Holy Spirit throughout the day so you can minister Christ's life to those He may bring in to contact with you.

Women or wives should have an education so that in case of an emergency she could carry on. Many times men marry before they have completed their education. Therefore, there will be some wives who will need to work during a certain period of marriage if her husband decides to complete his education. This, consequently, will enable him to be the sole provider in the home, making her time of working only a temporary situation.

In being educated it is obvious that the male and female have EQUAL ability and capability to increase their intellect and succeed in this world. However, it is also obvious that in a marriage relationship, the wife must take the submissive role. She should have the freedom to share her ideas and intellectual knowledge with her husband but enough faith to look to him for final decisions, keeping him in the leadership position so that he will feel that she thinks he is capable of handling his leadership role.

Chapter Twenty-One

Handling Money

The husband-wife attitudes toward the handling of the household income and budget need to be in agreement just as much as any other area in their marriage.

Who should handle the money? First of all, we cannot lay down any hard and fast rules, as each household is a unique situation. However, we can establish some general principles in line with our basic role as husband or wife.

Have you ever heard a wife say something like this: "We bought this stove with MY money." The immediate implication is a divided financial situation with two different decision-making "heads" which, nine times out of ten, leads to arguments and, for sure, plays havoc with the male ego.

For the sake of unity and the fact that the husband is the head of the home, it is best for him to accept his headship in this area and for the household income, checking and savings accounts, to be classified as OUR money. But also, for the sake of harmony in the relationship, it is good for husband and wife to have open communication in this area, to the point that there can be a mutual agreement in HOW you plan to spend and save your money.

Ideally, it is the husband's responsibility to support the family, to provide the money, to manage the main budget and to make the *final* decisions on how, when and where it is spent. The wife's responsibility should be to support his financial plan and manage the household budget IF he gives it to her to manage. Many men give a portion of the paycheck to their wives— enough to operate the household budget.

I would suggest that he doesn't hand you the whole responsibility of the budget. If he should hand you the responsibility of making the decisions of bill paying, and perhaps trying to decide what to do when there isn't enough money to pay all of the bills or how much should be saved, it could place you in a pressure situation. It may not be realized right away, but after a long period of time it can cause a great deal of resentment in your attitude toward your husband. When he hands you his responsibility, sometimes we, as "wife," are deceived into keeping it because we know that we have the ability and educated capability of handling it and doing a good job. However, just because we are capable of doing it doesn't mean it is expedient that we do so.

I would like to insert here that it is good to operate in your God-given role of woman-wife. The world sometimes puts down role playing, but in accordance with God's plan we have a role as "good wife" to fulfill; otherwise, God never would have made a woman and could have just had a world full of "Adams"—He could have just kept creating men at His will. The point is, don't be afraid to fulfill your role, even if you *feel* you are just "role playing." God will honor your faith in doing your part to bring Divine Order into your home.

If your husband delegates the checkbook responsibility to you, try to see that it remains on a bookkeeping level, where he is making the decisions about what, where and when to pay, and you write the checks and mail them. Let him make the decisions while you fulfill the role of helpmeet. You are taking on this job to save him the thirty minutes that it often takes to sit down, write the checks out, put them in envelopes, stamp them, mail them and keep the checkbook balanced with the bank statement. An arrangement like this keeps him in the leadership position. You can still help him with it, but keep your position as his helpmeet. He'll feel better, and you will too.

Some men do all the decision-making and bookkeeping in the household, giving the wife the money she needs to buy groceries, clothing for the family and miscellaneous items. Hopefully this man, even though he is doing all the work on the budget, is taking time to communicate with his wife so that they are in agreement, she is expressing her ideas and ultimately feels she has a part in making this plan work successfully.

Nonetheless, be a dollar stretcher. Help him maintain the budget. Don't mess up the budget because you found a "good deal" at the store today and you just couldn't pass it up! BE A DOLLAR STRETCHER.

Sometimes differences over finances can be solved by making two separate budgets (one for him and one for you). You'll have to discuss this with him, but sometimes this can be the solution to many arguments.

When I had the total responsibility of handling the finances, I realized I needed to return Bill's leadership position to him in this area. I had to crucify my pride. I had to say, "Here, Bill, is the checkbook. I realize I have tried to take this financial responsibility away from you, and I would like to offer it back to you." We hadn't had a disagreement or anything. I simply had realized what was happening. I wanted him to know I could give it to him to do so. I had recognized in my own heart that it was becoming a prideful thing with me, and it had also allowed him to release his leadership to me in this area. I admit, there were some reservations in my heart at the beginning because I thought, "What if he makes a mistake? What if he writes checks and subtracts it and it doesn't balance? What if the statement comes back and something is wrong?" I had to deal with this, these attitudes of lack of faith in him and my pride! It is easier when you are young and haven't had to deal with a lot of poor attitudes and emotions, but older married women who have held this responsibility perhaps for fifteen or twenty years, and sometimes without Jesus in their life, will find giving the checkbook back to their husband a lot harder. However, you need to be willing to do it, knowing that he may make some mistakes. At this point if he does give the checkbook back to you, I'm sure you could accept it on a "helpmeet" basis.

Some of us wives who have been self-centered and prideful are usually right there with our mouth, making sure he has our opinion of how it should be done. "Do it this way, this way, this way!" We stay after them. We don't want them to make any mistakes. We don't want anyone to know he isn't perfect! Let the responsibility be his. It will help him know you have faith and confidence in his leadership ability, and it will make him feel good.

Remember this: If God gives *you* the freedom to choose between right and wrong, shouldn't you as a wife be able to allow your husband the freedom to choose right or wrong?

Now it may be that your husband won't take responsibilities in areas such as this. There are some men who won't. They have been so "hammered down" in their past lives with statements like, "You are going to fail," "You won't make it," or "You don't have it in you." They have had failure ministered to them, and it has made them terrified of making mistakes. The male ego part of his soul has been pushed down to such a point that he has no confidence in himself.

If you have been the type of wife who has cut your husband to shreds with your tongue, it means you have a lot of work to do in rebuilding his confidence. It's a slow process building him up in his soulish area to the point where you can suggest a responsibility here and a responsibility there that he may be willing to take on.

DON'T NAG! Remember a nag is someone who says something more than once. Minister to him. It's got to be a *body-soul ministry* on your part. Let the Lord Jesus, through you, restore these things to his life—in those areas where he feels he has no confidence. Tell him with your mouth, voice to him (by faith) your confidence in him and point out to him all the ways he is successful and pleasing to you and your family. Then once he does start taking responsibilities, be sure to tell him how much you appreciate him taking that responsibility off your shoulders. For instance, tell him what a good provider he is. It took me twenty years of married life before I was free enough in my soul to say with my mouth, "Honey, you've been a good provider."

Even when we were in the world, my husband always took good care of us as far as material things were concerned. He always provided enough to keep the bills paid. Everything was always taken care of one way or another. He was a good provider. But never, not once, did I ever say with my mouth, "I really appreciate the fact that you have been a good provider in our home." When I realized what I had been doing (or rather, not doing), I went to my husband and said, "I really appreciate the way you've been a good provider for us all of our married life." He was like a little boy. He just "ate up my words" because he appreciated me telling him that. I had thought it in my mind, that I appreciated him, but I had never *given life to the words*. It's just like the Proverb says—your words can either be life or death. It is in the little things in the everyday, common situations in living that you can continuously minister life, or you can continuously minister death.

Chapter Twenty-Two

Be Pretty and Feel Good

Knowing how a *man* feels helps a woman to see the role her body plays in completing her man. We find that men have a *need* to feel masculine.

One way we can help our man feel masculine is to minister to him with our feminine body. This need to feel masculine is a natural need that he has in his body. God has made him this way, just as He has made you to be feminine and need to feel that way.

Concerning our own bodies, in 1 Corinthians 3:16 –17 (RSV) it says:

"Do you not know that you are God's temple, and that God's Spirit dwells in you? If anyone destroys God's temple, he will destroy Him, for God's temple is holy, and that temple you are."

That's speaking of your body—you are a temple! In 1 Corinthians 6:20 it says:

"You were bought for a price—purchased with a preciousness and paid for, made His own. So then, honor God and bring glory to Him in your body."

Let's not get so "spiritually minded" that we forget we are still in our bodies. Our bodies are to be of "earthly good!"

The care of our body is one thing most of us have heard a lot about since the first day of kindergarten. Our educational system has done a good job of teaching us to take care of our bodies. However, some of us when we become independent, forget those very basic, fundamental principles. Some of these principles even college girls groan about because they would rather not have to go through such courses as physical education or aerobics programs. Yet we have learned that an exercise program of some kind is something which should be carried through the rest of our lives, keeping the body in such good condition that it can glorify God.

It is important to feel good. We'd like to have a fresh appearance and the good health that goes along with the good looks. You know, a man wants a woman who looks and is genuinely happy, and you can't be happy or look happy if your body doesn't feel good. If you feel tired and run-down all of the time, he isn't going to be convinced that you are genuinely happy. As a husband, his efforts in leading, providing and protecting are ministering to you and taking care of you. If he isn't getting a positive response from your body, then he is going to begin thinking that he has failed! Right? So we have to ask ourselves: Are we overweight? Do we have flabby muscles? How about poor posture? Is there a lack of energy? Do we always look tired? Do we have physical disorders?

If the answer to any of these questions is yes, then I would be apt to say that your body is not under subjection to your spirit, and in your soulish nature you have lost your motivation. Did you know that a man really expects his wife to maintain the same good figure she had when he married her? (Oh my!) It's up to us to maintain. Right? I suppose you might want to say this is a very mundane thing, but it is really what he expects. I know for a fact that I, for one, don't expect my husband to "grow" one of these big potbellies that we see on so many men soon after marriage. I don't want that. I don't expect it from him, so I know he doesn't expect me to "blossom out" in places where I haven't "blossomed" before!

Let's see what we can do to obtain a fresh and vibrant appearance. First, we should get enough SLEEP. The body and soul react differently when we have had enough sleep. When we are rested, our mind functions more efficiently, our reactions and emotions are more controlled and we *feel* like taking time to exercise. For these reasons, it's really important that we have proper rest. It's for the health of the body and the well-being of the soul. It allows both of these areas to function properly. Did you know that rest also affects your sexual reactions to your husband? If you are tired...did you ever find yourself in the bathroom, taking an extra long time putting curlers in your hair, brushing your teeth, putting lots and lots of cream on your face...and by the time you came to bed, he was asleep? And you were oh, *so glad!* You love him, but you couldn't have cared less that night because you had let your body get run down. Doctors suggest to women that if they find themselves without enough strength to even hug their husbands at bedtime, they should take an afternoon nap for a half hour to an hour. An hour will completely restore you. It's surprising what it will do for you. (However, if you are on a good exercise program, you will usually find you have so much energy you will not need the nap.) I went through a period in my life when the children were young, where I was so drained by the time dear Hubby came home, I was exhausted. (And who has strength to do any body ministry to him? You've body-ministered all day long!) I had to learn how and when to rest. The *how* and when is different for each person and can only be worked into your day by you.

The second point is EXERCISE. Exercise does

produce energy. Proverbs 31:17 says:

"She girds herself with strength [spiritual, mental, and physical fitness for her God given task] and makes her arms strong and firm."

Setting aside a special time just for you to exercise is important. Plan a regular schedule of walking, jogging or tennis, or join a health club or just do exercises in your living room to some lively music. Do whatever suits you best, but *do something!* You'll feel great!

The third point I would make is to DRINK plenty of WATER, EAT NUTRITIOUSLY and get a lot of FRESH AIR. It's surprising what a little walk around the block will do for you in the middle of your morning chores. It will really change your entire outlook on life. Simply go outside and take a look at God's creation instead of the dirty floor or the sink full of dishes. (But don't forget to come back!) Six to eight glasses of water a day is the usual recommendation. There are plenty of good books out on nutrition to help you learn how to properly balance your intake of protein, vegetables, fruits and so forth. Your energy level can take a real low dive when you starve your body of the nutrients it needs.

Another important thing is to learn to RELAX when you are working, as well as when you are playing. This is something I'm still working on. Taking care of my home and my family is something I really like to do, but it is difficult sometimes to make myself relax in it since the Lord is still helping me win the battle over perfectionism. When I'm working, I'm just "gung-ho," and I really want to "get with it." I forget to relax and enjoy it. Relax does not necessarily mean "slow down." Oftentimes it is our relaxed attitude while working that will allow it to be a joy.

Having a healthy mental attitude, then, is part of this vibrant, fresh appearance also. Our soul attitudes and our emotions play a great part in the body's well-being.

Remember this: your husband and your children

want you to look and feel vibrant, alive and happy. As I said before, your husband is working toward this end. He wants to make you happy and meet your needs, and he needs a positive response from you. He wants you to look vibrant and look alive.

Don't forget to tell your face to smile. In my home I have a mirror over my kitchen sink because I've had a terrible time in this area. It's not hard for me to smile outside my home, but when I'm in my own home, it seems like my mind begins to organize and fret about getting everything done. This can be a very bad thing.

In our home, it became so bad that one day my son said, "You know, Mommy, I wish you were like Mrs. Long."

Surprised, I said, "Mrs. Long?"

"Yeah, she's happy, and she smiles all the time!"

That hit me hard. That was why he liked her. It really spoke to me. I bought a mirror and put it over my sink because it seemed as though I spent most of my time in the kitchen. Looking at myself reminds me to smile and sometimes it reminds me to fix myself up. Sparkling eyes go along with that smile. When you look at someone and you look into their eyes, it's not hard to read them. This is important. Don't just try to put a fake smile on your mouth. The smile has to start with your eyes, and it *has* to be real. Determine within yourself to look great for your family.

During the course of time in which the Lord was helping me begin to straighten out my priorities, I made a checklist to give each member in our family. There were twenty-five items listing things a homemaker is expected to do such as: have a clean bathroom, a clean kitchen, shiny floors, house cleaned throughout, beds changed often, laundry washed and ironed, mending caught up, good meals cooked, closets and drawers in order and so forth. Along with these things were six other points.

I asked my husband to take this list first and to

choose six items putting them in order of their importance to him. Then I gave the same list to our younger son, and then to our older son. Amazingly, they all chose the same six items! The items were distributed a little differently, but they were still the same six things.

This is the list of things that my husband chose, in order of his first priorities:

1. Mother happy, good-natured and rested. (That was also my younger son's first priority.)

2. Mother's appearance attractive and neat.

3. The house picked up. (It didn't have to be shiny, but picked up.)

4. Mom spend time with Dad. (My son put this down too—I thought that was pretty neat coming from my younger son!)

5. Mom spend time with children.

6. A good-smelling house.

Those six things, and I thought WOW! Here I had been knocking myself out, making sure that every drawer was straightened and that everything was in perfect shape all the time. Me and my perfectionist attitude had been leaving my family out in these particular areas they had picked from the list. You know, it was becoming obvious to me all along that they weren't so much concerned about what I did or accomplished as they were about ME. Of course, I had asked the Lord to show me, and when you ask the Lord to show you something, He does. So don't ever ask Him unless you want to know.

I was beginning to see that what my husband wanted was a wife, not just a housekeeper. My children wanted a happy mom they could talk to. It dawned on me one day that a man can hire a housekeeper to clean his house, but he cannot hire another wife. You know, sometimes we make ourselves so much of a housekeeper and a maid that we aren't a wife. It takes a lot of wisdom from the Lord, a lot of physical strength and a lot of prayer, but the Lord can bring us into a beautiful balance in our daily living so that we can be a good wife, mom and friend.

Chapter Twenty-Three

Be Feminine

As little girls grow up into mature, feminine, beautiful womanhood, they depart from the more carefree and perhaps careless beauty habits of childhood. We find that with the coming of physical maturity we are required to take a new look at ourselves. First, we are going to talk about a face that can sell you, the inner fulfilled, peaceful, joyful YOU. Initially it is your face and eyes that will present that appealing part of you to your husband, to your children and to your friends. We want to be an appealing, if not beautiful, representative of Christ. We want to be God's beautiful woman. We've been through the "kookykid" look, the "though chic" look and the "realist's natural" look. I wonder how many of us really want to be called a "Plain Jane" or a "Sad Sally," a "Listless Looking Lil" or a "Drab Dora." Most of us have had to learn by experience that as we grow up, we need to begin to think about a new face for us.

Age makes it necessary for us to work at keeping

that fresh and vibrant look that we had in our youth, and we should want to keep it for our husbands. You need to make him feel that he is really keeping you happy. It should show in your face. It is important that we not think, "Oh, I can let it slip this morning. I'll just brush my teeth and say, 'Here I am, World!'"

After we leave college, and sometimes while we're still in college, we begin to change, so it is then that we need to start thinking about a new face. Maybe not just for our man, but for our careers. We want to present ourselves as vital, energetic, pleasant and happy. We should desire to enhance our natural beauty.

To achieve that look of "natural beauty" I have some ideas I want to mention. The first idea is to make our facial skin and complexion more perfect. That doesn't mean you have to use a lot of pancake makeup, but there are liquid makeups which smooth out facial blemishes and add color. Hopefully you will become skilled enough in applying this makeup that you do not give in to an artificial look. In fact, "artificialness" is the look we want to stay away from and is a look most men dislike. We want to look naturally beautiful.

After putting on a base makeup, next comes the blush, or rouge. There are different ways we can learn to use blush to enhance the natural beauty of our face. To keep a fresh, young look, it's important to remember not to just touch up the cheeks, but the nose, the forehead and the chin as well, giving a youthful glow.

There are lots and lots of books and magazines on the market racks today that can teach us how to use makeup to our individual advantage. I've seen some good "before" and "after" shots in these magazines in which the transformation is incredible, even making it hard to believe it's the same girl.

Next on the agenda are eyelashes. They need to be accentuated and usually made darker. Some people have naturally dark eyelashes; therefore, all the enhancement they may need is a little curling. That "wide-eyed" look not overdone, but enough to help you look sparkling and happy, is an advantage. Eye shadow is good also, being used to accentuate your eyes and your eye color (unless your clothing decides what color you want to use). Remember soft colors, not overdone, give the soft look.

Eyebrows, I think, should be natural-looking brows, and again, helping to give that "wide-eyed" look. Some women are overly endowed with bushy brows, having to pluck and shape them, while others with very light brows may have to use an eyebrow pencil to darken them. Experiment to see what best suits *your* face. After forty it is best to shape your eyebrows so that the outside end of the brow goes straight out or slightly up and never down.

Your lipstick should be what is suitable to you, your complexion and dress. I think it is important to work with your complexion in the lipstick area. For example, if you are fair be very careful when wearing dark shades as harsh colors may tend to give you that "Jezebel" appearance.

The overall look, then, is to bring out and enhance our natural beauty. It's not good to try to be something or someone we aren't. This is what the last generation of women went to seed on. In the late sixties college girls said that everything had to be *real*. They wanted "reality." That was the issue. The style was no makeup, hair parted straight down the middle and everything just "doin' what comes naturally." Well, there is a balance between overdoing and underdoing. Remember that balance is what each of us needs to find for herself. It's up to *you* what type of look you want and what you feel enhances *your* natural beauty.

But no matter how much we work at it, there is one thing we can never do and that is hide fatigue on our faces. No matter how much makeup you use, you will never be able to hide a lack of sleep or a lack of good care for your overall body. There is no amount of makeup in the world that will hide all of that. You need to be responsible to your entire being—spirit, soul and body—for a totally beautiful you.

What is femininity then? It's a gentle, tender quality; something we want to achieve. It is achieved by accentuating the differences between man and woman. A man feels masculine in the presence of a feminine woman, and *he likes this feeling*. He wants to feel like a man, and he wants you to look and feel like a woman. This is part of BODY ministry. It makes both of you feel good. So we ask, "How can we *be* feminine? How can we *look* feminine?"

To begin with, the type of clothing and colors we wear have a direct effect on our look of femininity. We should avoid fabrics, colors and styles that are masculine. Some of the things to be careful of are using drab colors and bold, heavy materials such as tweeds, heavy corduroy and herringbone stripes which tend to be very masculine. If you do use those fabrics, you have to be very careful how you handle them to keep femininity coming across. The very tailored look can be very sophisticated and feminine if accentuated with scarves, flowers and jewelry or a soft, fluffy blouse.

As for colors, femininity is easier to put across with beautiful prints, pastels or bright colors. Feminine fabrics such as silk, lace and organdies are very nice. Some dacron polyesters are very feminine also. Chiffons, velvets, satins and furs are all very good to use. Feminine styles are easily depicted in dresses or skirts, and, again, almost any style or color of clothing can be made more feminine by adding ruffles, ribbons, scarves, bows, flowers and jewelry. You can make a tailored neck more feminine, for example, simply by adding a bow. It can give a totally different look, a look of femininity versus masculinity.

Another thing we can do to help show our feminine nature is to avoid wearing pants *all* the time. It does something to your feminine feeling to wear skirts. Please note that I am not saying that a woman should *never* wear pants. It is, however, obvious that a woman will automatically walk, stand and sit in a more feminine manner when she is wearing a skirt. This also brings up the question of the doctrine in some denominations which says women must not wear pants at all.

Let's go to the Bible. In Deuteronomy 22:5 it says:

"The woman shall not wear that which pertains to a man, neither shall a man put on a woman's garment; for all that do so are an abomination to the Lord your God."

Here the Word says we aren't to wear anything that pertains to a man, *appearing masculine.* Does that include slacks, casual pants and feminine pantsuits? I hardly think so. If you saw a man in a ladies-styled pantsuit, you would say, "That's feminine!" That clothing does not pertain to a man. It does pertain to a woman. I think women who offend in wearing pants are the ones who *continuously* let themselves *look* masculine: wearing masculine-looking shirts, or pants with the big flies that are definitely masculine. There isn't anything in the Word that states, "Don't wear pants." It is saying don't look like a man. Look like a woman, and you can. You can look like a very feminine woman in pants. However, it's not a good thing to wear them *all* the time, especially if you want to get into a more feminine attitude yourself. Did you ever notice how different your mannerisms are when you wear pants all the time? Many times I have noticed that when I have worn pants that I am altogether too free with my legs when sitting and I walk like a man with long, careless strides, mannerisms which are not flattering.

If a woman is doing yard work, farm work, factory work and so forth, the appropriate dress may be pants. However, even in blue jeans and a shirt a woman can make her appearance and mannerisms feminine.

We know that the Word was written for all people in every part of the earth. Does the man in Africa or the

Orient who wears a skirt become feminine? Of course not. In his culture he dresses in a skirt according to that dress pertaining to men in his country.

A good rule to set is to do all things in moderation. A woman's hair should be soft and feminine, makeup should be simple, making us a beautiful representative of the inner woman. When we first came to the Lord, we went to a little Pentecostal church. I looked around, and the first thing I noticed was that most of the women had no makeup on and they had big, tight hairdos. I thought, "Oh Lord, if You want me to look like this, I'll take off my makeup and I'll change my hair. I'm willing to do this because I want to do everything You want me to do. EVERYTHING!!" I prayed about it, and I searched my heart to see if there was vanity or pride or anything unpleasing to the Lord. I looked at myself one morning in the mirror before making up my face and said, "Lord, how could anyone look at that and think there was anything really good inside?" It convinced me. If I'm beautiful on the outside, or at least feel I am pleasing to look at, it helps me to forget about me, and I can concentrate on presenting the One who is in me, Jesus.

In 1 Timothy 2:9–10 Paul was speaking about adornment:

"Also [I desire] that women should adorn themselves modestly and appropriately and sensibly in seemly apparel not with [elaborate] hair arrangement or gold or pearls or expensive clothing, but by doing good deeds—that is, deeds in themselves good, and for the good and advantage of those contacted by them—as befits women who profess reverential fear for and devotion to God."

First Peter 3:4–5 says the same thing:

"But let it be the inward adorning and beauty of the hidden person of the heart, with the incorruptible and unfading charm of a gentle and peaceful spirit, which (is not anxious or wrought up, but) is very precious in the sight of God. For it was

thus that the pious women of old who hoped in God were (accustomed) to beautify themselves, and were submissive to their husbands—adapting themselves to them as themselves secondary and dependent upon them."

We believe the Lord Jesus Christ has authority over us. He has the authority to regulate our apparel, as well as everything else that pertains to us. And within that regulation, we should be trying to please our husband in the way that we dress as well as remembering the things which we spoke about in the previous chapters concerning our feminine charm and gentle, peaceful spirit.

These two particular Scripture verses also deal with the temptations women have today. Fashions have great power over women. For example, we have come out of the era of miniskirts. Perhaps you remember. Many even "good" Christian women completely lost their modesty and shocked even the most worldly men by wearing extremely short miniskirts. All for the sake of fashion!

These verses also speak of being tempted to spend too much time on ourselves, plaiting (or braiding) the hair. Long hair can take too much time, especially if it is really being prepared or cared for properly. Time and modest, appropriate apparel is what he is speaking of in this verse. It is possible to spend too much time on apparel and on the hair.

Some people say, "The Bible says for women to have long hair." No, 1 Corinthians 11:4 is the verse under scrutiny here, and it says that long hair is the glory of a woman. If a man has long hair, making him look feminine, it is a shame to him. That's what it says. It doesn't say that a woman has to have extra long hair. The Word is stressing the difference between *femininity* and *masculinity*. Peter wasn't saying, "Don't fix your hair, and don't wear gold," because if he WAS saying that in verse 2, then in verse 3 he was saying, "Don't wear any clothes!" Isn't it true that if we, as women, would spend as much time fasting and praying as we do "fixing up," we would really be spiritual giants? We all can see this, and I'm sorry to say that some of us have been spiritually negligent.

But what we are after is balance. That is the point Peter is making in this Scripture verse. We don't have to look like witches, nor do we have to look like Jezebels, but there is a modest and appropriate balance. We don't want to spend all of our time on the outward man, with no time for the inner man. We want to *first* adorn the inner man, so that we receive inner peace, and then adorn the outer man. We want to be tender and feminine and gentle. So let's put the emphasis on the humble spirit rather than on the dress. Some of the "holiest" dressing women I've known have proven to be altogether mean and utterly self-righteous. It doesn't have a thing to do with the outward adornment, does it? It is what comes out of the mouth and heart.

How does she minister? Does she minister life? We know that men have picked up these Scripture verses and made traditions out of them, but it is important that we realize all Scripture verses must be interpreted in the light of other Scripture passages. Don't ever pull out one verse and base a doctrine on it without confirming it with passages elsewhere in the Bible. If it is truly God's Word, there will always be other Scripture verses to confirm it.

Let's talk about feminine manner. Our manner has to do with our hands and making them graceful—having gentle hands. When we walk, walk with our head up, our thighs forward and with small steps. It's not feminine to gallop down the street like a man. Our talk should be gentle, not harsh. We need to have sweet voices. Our laughs should be feminine, not roaring, and throwing our heads back like a man. Nor is it feminine to slap your legs. Facial expression is another thing. Watch yourself. Be soft and feminine. Beware of tight lips and a frown (it makes wrinkles).

Also regarding various types of jobs around the house, I would suggest that you try not to do a heavy job in front of a man unless you can do it in a feminine manner. Sometimes out of necessity we have to do them. There are ways to work and come off looking like Tarzan, and in contrast you can do it so well that you look like Jane—even if you are left with some of his responsibilities. Maybe you are expected to drive a tractor, seed a field, mow the lawn, shovel up all the dirt for your new spring garden or paint the house. Whatever it is, try to keep your femininity. Some of these jobs can be enjoyable. I know that gardening can be a good excuse to enjoy the outside. I'm not knocking it. I enjoy painting inside—in the bedrooms, in redoing the bathroom and so forth—but I also have realized that you can lose your femininity and make your husband feel like he is less than a man by taking on his jobs out of your impatience, thinking he can't do them soon enough or well enough to suit you. Resentment usually follows that type of situation, so it's better to avoid your impatience and apply some "soul ministry" as we discussed previously.

Women are made quite physically different than men. Peter brought this out in 1 Peter 3:7:

"In the same way you married men should live considerately with [your wives], with an intelligent recognition [of the marriage relation], honoring the woman as [physically] the weaker...."

I have always felt honored when my husband or any other man did things for me to show his protection of me as a female. Besides feeling honored, it made me feel feminine, and I'm sure it made him feel more masculine. Remember, the feminine manner makes the man feel manly, a feeling he desires and needs to feel completed.

Chapter Twenty-Four

The Shock Absorber

An eighty-year-old woman came up to me after I had spoken about sex in the Christian marriage at a ladies' luncheon. She told me how excited she was that I had spoken on this subject to the young married women who were present. Then sorrowfully she stated that if she had known fifty years ago some of the things which I had shared, it would have changed her whole attitude and helped her marriage so much. Her statement encouraged me to continue sharing on this subject.

The more we speak on this subject and counsel married couples the more aware we have been made of wrong attitudes, misinformation, lack of knowledge and the downright misinterpretation of Scripture and blatant perversion of the sex act itself.

I think that many have been deceived by the clever mass media's impressions and projections of sex for our lives today, and unless we are grounded firmly in the Word, we really don't know HOW or WHAT to think in

Christian terms about our sexual relationship with our husband.

I'll never forget the day a very particularly wonderful person in my life came and told me that she thought we were to have fun in our sex relationship with our husband. It seemed like the Holy Spirit just took that one word, *fun*, and exploded something inside of me that had not been touched before. It really helped to release my mind to a new avenue in which the Lord could teach me to minister to my husband. The Holy Spirit then showed me this particular area in my life where I had allowed myself to be bound by unfounded guilts and fears. Unfounded because the guilt and fears were based on past sins which had been confessed, forgiven and forgotten by God. At that moment the light of Jesus began to meet my need, and we started renewing my mind by His Word and His way.

To be a successful, accountable Christian wife it is our responsibility to learn how to have right attitudes in our sexual relationship with our husband. We need to know the joys and the natural responses to a healthy, happy sexual relationship, and knowing how to communicate freely our sexual needs to our husband is imperative.

From time to time, sitting under the hair dryer at the beauty shop, I have thumbed through the many ladies' magazines. I enjoy keeping up with the styles and reading the beauty tips, diets and exercise routines. It inspires me to keep myself beautiful for my husband. However, much to my astonishment, I noticed that in these ladies' magazines they were boldly exclaiming their opinions on how to find sexual satisfaction. They were recommending to women, in general, that they should or could use different methods, such as masturbation, to help them experience an orgasm, stating that many women had never experienced an orgasm and some don't even know there is such a thing. Other articles openly discussed oral sex as a *natural* means of sexual satisfaction. These articles caused my mind to reel and my stomach to feel sick. I could hardly believe what I was reading and here it was openly discussed in the most popular and supposedly "sophisticated" ladies' magazines—where anyone and everyone could read it. No wonder couples are finding such bizarre problems in their marriages!

One of the magazines, which I know is highly popular with girls who are high-school-age and older, ran several articles on living together without marriage, condoning it and implying: Whatever feels good, do it! Of course, the underlying pull and temptation to sin is seeking SELF-SATISFACTION...at any cost!

Self, self...we know that in our Christian walk, no matter what area that we are in—spirit, soul or body—it has to be a *loving* walk and a *giving* walk. As long as our relationship, sexually and otherwise, with our husband is a giving one (you wanting to give yourself 100 percent to him and him giving himself 100 percent to you), then we are going to be successful, and we are going to have victory in all areas of our relationship.

The Bible itself classifies masturbation, oral sex and sex without marriage as sin, that is: fornication, adultery, homosexuality, immorality, sexual looseness, a sin against our own body, sexual impurity, vile affections, degrading passions, unnatural relations or shameful acts.

"But the person who is united to the Lord becomes one spirit with Him. Shun immorality and all sexual looseness—flee from impurity [in thought, word or deed]. Any other sin which a man commits is one outside the body, but he who commits sexual immorality sins against his own body. Do you not know that your body is the temple—the very sanctuary—of the Holy Spirit Who lives within you, Whom you have received [as a Gift] from God? You are not your own, you were bought for a price— purchased with a preciousness and paid for, made

His own. So then, honor God and bring glory to Him in your body" (1 Cor. 6:17–20).

"Therefore God gave them up in the lusts of their [own] hearts to sexual impurity, to the dishonoring of their bodies among themselves, abandoning them to the degrading power of sin....For this reason, God gave them over and abandoned them to vile affections and degrading passions. For their women exchanged their natural function for an unnatural and abnormal one; and the men also turned from natural relations with women and were set ablaze (burned out, consumed) with lust for one another, men committing shameful acts with men and suffering in their own bodies and personalities the inevitable consequences and penalty of their wrong doing and going astray, which was [their] fitting retribution" (Rom. 1:24,26–27).

I have heard some so-called Spirit-filled women say, "You can do anything you want on the marriage bed because the Bible says the marriage bed is undefiled." Well, I do not believe this is the correct interpretation of that Scripture verse, and I know for a fact the misinterpretation of this verse has been used to try to justify oral sex as a means of satisfaction.

Let's read what the Word says in Hebrews 13:4:

"Let marriage be held in honor—esteemed worthy, precious, [that is], of great price and especially dear—in all things. And thus let the marriage bed be (kept undishonored), undefiled; for God will judge and punish the unchaste (all guilty of sexual vice) and adulterous."

As you can see, the Word does not say the marriage bed *is* undefiled—it says *keep it* undefiled. Undefiled means free from *sin*.

Why should we have to revert to the unnatural acts and methods (oral sex) of lesbians and homosexuals to find sexual satisfaction? It is sheer deception from the devil to think that we would have to use such methods.

There is a tiny book written for Christian couples entitled *You Can Find Sexual Satisfaction* by Harry McGee. This booklet is great for those who need some teaching or information on sexual satisfaction in their marriage.

While we are talking about the sex drive, I would like to insert here what I feel is an answer to a question often asked by widows, divorcees and single men and women: "How do I cope with my sex drive? I know that satisfying myself (by masturbation) is wrong, but what can I do? I feel so tormented! And I don't have a mate to satisfy this need."

The answer came to me after teaching a session on "Love and Sex in the Christian Marriage." A widow came to me and said, "When I first became a widow I was sorely tempted to masturbate because I could see no other way for me to release this sex drive, and knowing in my heart that I did not wish to remarry I felt almost desperate. I began praying about it. I thought of Paul. He said he had received a gift from God in the matter of self-control."

"I wish that all men were like I myself am [in this matter of self-control]. But each has his own special gift from God, one of this kind and one of another." **(1 Cor. 7:7)**

She said, "I asked God for this gift, and He gave it to me! Truly, I am no longer tormented. He provided a way for me to escape." (see 1 Cor. 10:13).

I had a hallelujah time right there because I knew here was a scriptural answer for a great need in the lives of many people. Since then I have shared this verse with many divorcees, singles and widows who desired to not sin in this area. They have acted on the Word, laid claim to this gift and with much joy and relief have received the help they needed.

Obviously there is a wrong approach to sex, but there is also a right one. God means for us to have a healthy sex relationship, knowing among other things, that in a marriage it reduces friction. I can remember when I thought I was just being *used* as a "sleeping pill," when my husband wanted sexual relations. And naturally because I would fellowship with that thought the devil would see to it that resentment would follow. As I have said before, since my husband and I had lived fifteen years without Jesus Christ in our home, we were very much influenced by the devil and by the world. We were doing many things that were wrong and had taken many attitudes and influences into our spirits, our souls and our bodies that were abnormal. They were not true to the Word. But you know, as we renewed our minds with the Word of God, He showed us that we needed to change and that we had the POWER to change our attitudes and emotions.

The Lord finally got it through to me that a good sexual relationship was a very important part of my ministry to my husband, to his body area as a release, not only to him, but to me, too, and that it does act as a "shock absorber" in our daily living. There is not a marriage on the face of the earth that doesn't have to experience some kind of trials, tribulations, adjustments and adapting to each other's personality and each other's desire.

But God not only gave us this physical act as a shock absorber, He gave us a way to have physical unity in our bodies as well as in our soul area. We become emotionally involved in this act, don't we? When there is satisfaction on both the husband's and the wife's part, there is an emotional security built up in their soul areas which is very important to the marriage relationship.

So I emphasize here again that you are a triune person. You have to minister to your husband in the spirit, minister to his soul and minister to him in his body. If you fail in any one of those, then there is weakness. There is a place where the enemy can come in and break down your marriage. Relatively speaking then, you can become severely handicapped without a good, balanced sex life in your marriage.

If you are having some sex-related problems, don't give up because of *feelings* that you have. But remember because you are equal in the spirit with your husband, and God is always on the side of right, you have wonderful opportunities for wonderful victories.

Our attitudes toward submission and these Scripture verses which we've already talked about in Titus, Ephesians and others, those attitudes that you have toward submitting yourself to your husband in the spirit the soul and the body, will have a direct effect on your sexual relationship. In other words, if you're not willing to submit yourself to your husband in the kitchen, there is no way when you get to the bedroom at night that you can have a good sexual relationship. It just can't work because you get the feeling that he is using you, right? Keep in mind that God has ordained that if we choose to marry a man, we have a responsibility to abide by the rules and the rules are submission by love. If you choose to show love to him in the kitchen and in the living room and so forth, his reactions and actions in the bedroom will be different and you won't feel used.

"For the wife does not have [exclusive] authority and control over her own body, but the husband [has his rights], likewise also the husband does not have [exclusive] authority and control over his body, but the wife [has her rights]. Do not refuse and deprive and defraud each other (of your due marital rights), except perhaps by mutual consent for a time, that you may devote yourselves unhindered to prayer. But afterwards resume marital relations, lest Satan tempt you [to sin] through your lack of restraint of sexual desire" (1 Cor. 7:4–5).

I think that speaks really loud. "Do not refuse, deprive or defraud...."

Other things which will have a direct effect on your feelings of satisfaction or the success or failure of your sexual relationship are: feelings of guilt, unforgiveness of self or mate, broken spiritual relationship with God and lack of acceptance of yourself or mate. We have already discussed the solutions to each of these attitudes or emotions in previous chapters, so if you have problems in these areas, I suggest you backtrack.

The care of your body in preparation for physical contact with your husband is important. How your body looks, feels and how it smells has a great effect on his desire for you. I've had girls in my class that have come to me afterwards and said, "My mother never told me anything about personal hygiene—that I should clean myself in a certain way, that I can make myself smell good and don't have to smell like this." One young married girl came to me and said that her husband was groaning and moaning and that he didn't even want to be in the same bed with her, let alone touch her. So after finding out that she had a terrible vaginal odor, I gave her a few little personal hints on how to keep her body clean. I explained the purpose of a douche bag and in her case, the necessity of daily douching (in my opinion) with a couple of tablespoons of vinegar in a quart of water and taking a daily bath or shower. Daily douching may not be necessary and some doctors say not to. However, if there is a question in your mind or an indication of infection, I would definitely follow up with prayer for healing or professional advice.

Well, I truly become disappointed in the fact that mothers don't have a better relationship with their daughters and are not able to share with them the need to be beautiful on the outside so that Jesus can shine and minister through them. If you feel big, fat, ugly and unuseful, how can your attitude in bed be any different? If you don't like yourself in the kitchen, how are you going to like yourself in the bedroom, in bed with your husband? The enemy attacks there, too, you know. Just because you have turned out the lights and pulled up the covers doesn't mean the devil went away. He's still around.

A lady wrote to us after viewing our television program and said, "My husband was a pastor for thirty years, and he died of cancer. No one could understand why he died such a horrible death. He was a Spirit-filled man. Supposedly a godly man of faith and power." She found out after he died that he had committed adultery. She was writing her confession of resentment and bitterness and was trying to deal with it so she could be set free and put in right standing with God.

As I meditated on her situation I thought, "I wonder why his cancer was not healed. Was it because he was living in adultery?" I wanted to ask her, "Was it your fault? Were you not paying attention to him in the bedroom? Were you not satisfying his sexual needs? Were you the one that drove him to that other woman to commit adultery, to the end that he could not be healed because of his sin?" Of course, I didn't ask her but I wondered—was it her fault?

That is heavy. But this kind of situation is happening every day. My heart is crying out for women that are missing happiness, fulfillment and love because of a lack of knowledge and a lack of teaching.

I want you to know that God wants you to pray and ask Him how you as a wife can meet the sexual needs of your husband, and if you are not being satisfied, how God can help your husband meet your needs. God wants you to pray this way. He made you to have these needs. He made you the completed part of your husband. You completed him—he needs you! God wants you to be happy in this area, to find victory and fulfillment.

Mark 10:6–9 says:

"But from the beginning of creation God made them male and female. For this reason a man shall leave (behind) his father and his mother and be joined to his wife, and cleave closely to her (permanently). And the two shall become one flesh, so that they are no longer two, but one flesh. What therefore God has united—joined together—let not man separate or divide."

Summary

As you put God first in your life and renew your mind daily in the Word, the Holy Spirit will begin teaching you and making you aware of how you can be the *UltiMATE Woman.* He will point out the areas you need to change or improve. Wait on the Lord. Take time to develop your relationship with Him, just as you take time to develop your relationship with your husband. Minister to your husband: your spirit to his spirit, your soul to his soul, your body to his body.

The secret to success is **total commitment** to your love covenant, knowing that all things which are temporal are subject to change through the power of the Holy Spirit, in the name of Jesus and to the glory of our Father.

Scripture References

Genesis 1:26–27, 31
Genesis 2:18
Genesis 2:23–25
Genesis 3:16–19
Genesis 21:10–12
Deuteronomy 5:9
Deuteronomy 22:5
1 Samuel 1:21–22
1 Samuel 25
Nehemiah 8:10
Psalm 103:12
Psalm 118:6 –7
Proverbs 16:3
Proverbs 18:21–22
Proverbs 19:13
Proverbs 20:27
Proverbs 21:9
Proverbs 27:15
Proverbs 31:10–31
Isaiah 1:18
Isaiah 26:3
Isaiah 43:25
Jeremiah 31:34
Hosea 4:6
Micah 7:19
Matthew 7:2
Matthew 7:7
Matthew 12:34, 37
Mark 10:6–9
Mark 11:25
Mark 12:24, 30
Mark 14:3–9
Luke 8:1–3

Luke 8:21
John 4:7– 42
John 10:10
John 11
John 12
John 19:26
Acts 1:8
Acts 2:4
Acts 3:19
Romans 1:24–27
Romans 2:4
Romans 8:14–17, 26 –27
Romans 12:1–2, 9–10
Romans 16:1– 4, 6, 12
1 Corinthians 1:30
1 Corinthians 3:16 –17
1 Corinthians 5:7
1 Corinthians 6:17, 20
1 Corinthians 7:2–5
1 Corinthians 7:13–15
1 Corinthians 11:3, 7–9
1 Corinthians 11:16
1 Corinthians 12:8–10
1 Corinthians 13:4–7
1 Corinthians 14:1–2
1 Corinthians 14:13–15
1 Corinthians 15:39
2 Corinthians 5:21
Galatians 3:27–29
Galatians 4:4–7
Galatians 5:19–23
Ephesians 2:4–7
Ephesians 5:21–25

Ephesians 5:31, 33
Philippians 4:2–3
Philippians 4:8–9, 19
Colossians 3:18
1 Timothy 2:9–10
2 Timothy 2:15
Titus 2:3–5
Hebrews 10:14–24
Hebrews 13:4
1 Peter 3:1–7
1 John 3:2
2 John 2
Jude 20

A STUDY COMPANION FOR *The UltiMate Woman*

By *Bea Basansky*

This study companion is intended for use with *The UltiMate Woman*. It may be used for individual study. However, it is ideally used in a committed, weekly, small group setting.

Each section is designed to stimulate reading, study, reflection, discussion and growth. Some of the "how" and "why" questions will require creative thinking, even prayer, to answer.

Studies are divided into sections as follows:

PREPARATION—Outlined in the beginning of each study section are the primary Scripture references for that study.

REMEMBER—Words of encouragement especially for you!

QUESTIONS—Questions are drawn both directly from each chapter and from related material designed to stimulate thought and discussion.

RISK AND GROW—Trust requires vulnerability which is part of sharing one's personal thoughts and struggles with others. These exercises are opportunities for building individual and group trust.

JUST FOR FUN—This is used only once in the text and is as it says: "Just for fun!"

Send your order and payment to:

Bill Basansky Ministries
Love and Grace Fellowship
P.O. Box 7126
Fort Myers, FL 33911-7126

Phone: (813) 768-1300
Fax: (813) 768-0024

Name

Address

City   State   Zip(+4)

Telephone Number

Qty	Cat.	Title	Price	Total
	B30	*The Ultimate Woman*	8.00	
	B40	A Study companion for		
		The Ultimate Woman	4.00	
		Subtotal		
		Add 25% for Canadian		
		Add 10% Shipping & Handling ($1 min)		
		Grand Total		